STEVENSON AND EDINBURGH

By the same author

RETURN TO SCOTLAND
A WAYFARER IN POLAND
THE NOBLEST PROSPECT
SCOTTISH DELIGHT
A DINNER WITH THE DEAD
ESCAPE AND RETURN
STERN AND WILD
THE UNPOSSESSED
BY ME . . . . . (*A Shakespearean Study*)
A SMALL STIR (*in collaboration with James Bridie*)
ONE TRAVELLER RETURNS (*Play*)

EARLY "TRAVELS ON A DONKEY"

MORAY McLAREN

STEVENSON
AND
EDINBURGH

A CENTENARY STUDY

PR
5494
M35

LONDON
CHAPMAN & HALL
1950

Printed by The Alcuin Press, Welwyn Garden City, Herts.
Bound by G. & J. Kitcat, Ltd., London
Cat. No. 4141/4

INTRODUCTION

I HAVE long wanted to write this book, and freely admit that I have only made an excuse of this centenary to publish it. Until now I have been deterred by a reluctance to add anything to the large amount of literature on Robert Louis Stevenson, his writings, his life and his character. The contemplation of the many shelves of books devoted to these subjects in the public libraries dampened again and again my intermittent ardour.

However, as I read through these books from shelf to shelf, over a period of years, a conviction grew on me. It was this: no one had dealt properly and fully (from understanding and at any length) on what I believe to be the most formative influence in Stevenson's life—his native city. Of course, there were countless reminiscences about "R.L.S. and his Edinburgh days", many "glowing tributes" from prominent fellow-citizens written after his death, and hundreds of paragraphs in journals and, in correspondence, of genuine and heartfelt appreciation from lovers of Edinburgh. But none of these, valuable though they were, seemed to me to deal with the question, the answer to which I felt I dimly apprehended—Edinburgh and Stevenson? Stevenson and Edinburgh?

There was even less information or illuminating comment from English and American critics and biographers. The English, for all their delicate appreciation of Stevenson as an artist, tend to be ill-informed or condescending when writing about R.L.S. and his city. For the most part they seem to have looked upon Edinburgh as no more than a picturesque but accidental and provincial background to the early years of a man of genius. They usually under-estimate or wrongly estimate its influence on him. The Americans, on the other hand, in their writings on Stevenson have certainly not neglected R.L.S.'s birthplace. With that laborious industry, for which their literary scholars are noted, they have dug up a number of interesting and sometimes illuminating facts about Stevenson's youthful years in Edinburgh. Their treatment of and comments on these facts have been, in the eyes of most natives of the city, hopelessly wide of the mark.

Edinburgh is a very difficult place to know properly. It is only too easy for the visitor (even if he comes from no further than Glasgow) to think, on a short acquaintance, that he knows the city because he finds its dramatic appearance and certain obvious mannerisms of its inhabitants easy to grasp. He is mistaken. Americans, then, can scarcely be blamed if they have commented on Stevenson's Edinburgh background in a string of *clichés* and have viewed its human world, either in the present or in Victorian times, through a mass of popular misconceptions ready-made or acquired during a short stay.

Someone, I felt, ought to write a properly informed study on Stevenson and Edinburgh, someone who was not only well read in Stevenson but who knew Edinburgh, and not only Edinburgh, but the kind of Edinburgh from which Stevenson came. His contemporaries were all dead. Those few who remembered having met him, either did not know Edinburgh or were too old to write about it. No one of my own twentieth-century generation in Edinburgh seemed interested enough to undertake the task. Should I try it myself? I procrastinated. And then, with a suddenness that surprised me, the centenary of Stevenson's birth became imminent. I seized upon the excuse.

Having allowed myself the luxury of a preface, I would like to end by saying that I have tried to confine myself in this short book strictly to the subject in hand. I have not attempted to discuss Stevenson's character save in relation to Edinburgh, save in so far as he was influenced by his city. Any literary criticism in which I have indulged has been done with the same purpose. This means, of course, that I have omitted much about Stevenson's development as a man and as an artist.

One final point. It may seem to some that I have given a disproportionately large amount of space to Stevenson's rebellious peregrinations in the underworld of his city when he was a very young man. It may seem also that in so doing I have neglected other of his activities in Edinburgh—his friendship with the Fleeming Jenkins', his membership of the "Speculative Society" and so on. Let me explain myself. The Fleeming Jenkin household, R.L.S.'s amateur acting, even his speeches at the "Spec", have nothing very much to do with Edinburgh. They could have occurred in the life of any eager young literary-minded man anywhere. Moreover, they have been so exhaustively written about that there is no more information to add, few conclusions to be drawn from them. On the other hand, the solace that Stevenson found in Leith Walk, the Lothian Road and similar districts of Edinburgh has, in my opinion, never been understood, never properly accounted for.

I know that this side of his life has been the subject of much controversy, some muck-raking, and some indignant, well-meant, but blind denial. I know, too, that recent critics and biographers have passed over the controversy and its cause as not worth discussing. I cannot agree. I believe that this rebellion and escape against the background of Edinburgh by Stevenson was important to him, that it influenced him as a man and as an artist. I believe its influence remained with him to the end of his days. It is for this reason that I have devoted three chapters to an attempt to understand and account for this period of his Edinburgh life. Whether, in this portion of my book, I have been any more successful than those who have gone before me, is for the reader to judge. At any rate, I have thought the attempt worth while, and have enjoyed making it, and writing the results—in Edinburgh.

This book is as much about Edinburgh as it is about Stevenson.

M. McL.

CHAPTER I

In the year of R. L. Stevenson's birth, eighteen hundred and fifty, the top of the Calton Hill was the best place from which to see all Edinburgh. It still is. The unchangeable things are, of course, still there; and the view of them remains unobstructed —the hills, the Castle Rock, the nearby arm of the sea, the "cloud galleons" racing and bending across the wide tumultuous Scottish sky. The things, too, that man can change and that you can see from here he has not changed much. The general pattern of the late eighteenth- and early nineteenth-century New Town has been untouched. And any details of disfigurement are invisible from this eminence. It is true that in Princes Street, which runs directly below one and away from one, the squat little uniform Regency-type houses which some people disliked, but for which I who never saw them have a sentimental regret, have gone. In their place is a jumble of late-Victorian and Edwardian wealthy shop and hotel building. But from this height and this distance you can almost overlook if you cannot forgive that jumble. The great street is still as wide as ever it was and its site as noble. And if a large hotel disfigures the East End of it the blemish is blotted out by the romantic dignity of the rock and the Old Town behind it. Down by Holyrood the slums and the breweries still crowd and cluster. But they were crowding and clustering seventy years ago when Stevenson as a student looked from this place on this scene.

The Calton Hill view of Edinburgh was Stevenson's favourite prospect of the city from within the city. He devotes a chapter to it in his *Picturesque Notes on Edinburgh*. He makes the crucial incident in his most peculiarly Edinburgh story *The Misadventures of John Nicholson* happen upon this site, and devotes a long passage, composed towards the end of his life (when he was suffering most from homesickness) to a description of the sight of Edinburgh from this place at midnight. Any Edinburgh-born person who associates his love for his native city with the memory of Stevenson cannot but recall him when he stands upon this spot.

Standing here, and looking down upon a scene not very different from that which R.L.S. looked upon he might well wonder what R.L.S. would think were he to be, not only conjured up beside the spectator on this small hill, but taken down into the modern city itself. What would the student of 1870 think of the Edinburgh University students (now drawn from both sexes) and drawn also from even farther parts of the earth than in his days? When he was at the University a student from the Hebrides or the Norse Isles was considered remote. Now Chinese and African men and women are commonplace. What would the young man whose boyish passion for the toy theatre of Mr. Skelt was to haunt him all his life, whose youthful experience of the drama was confined to acting in Professor Fleeming Jenkin's amateur productions, what would he think of an Edinburgh in which there are half a hundred cinemas? What would the devotee of the puppet stage (with which as a child he was not allowed to play on the Sabbath) think of Princes Street filled with Sunday evening queues for the modern puppet show of the screen? What would the young writer with the incomparably acute ear for the nuances of Scottish speech make of the hideous half-American half-"keely" noises uttered by many of those who form these queues? And, speaking of speech, would he laugh at, or with, or would he enthusiastically support those partly serious, partly light-hearted young men who to-day are attempting to revive the glories of the ancient Scottish tongue? Would he be startled or delighted or just faintly amused if he were to see columns of correspondence in the once staid old *Scotsman* on the subject of the Lallans tongue—he who had used the word Lallans as an archaism seventy to eighty years ago? What would the highly Scottish writer of mid-Victorian days think of modern Scottish Nationalism? What would "Velvet coat" of the old Leith Walk think of the *Palais de danse*? What would he think of the influence of radio, aeroplanes, motor-cars and all the rest of it on Edinburgh—Edinburgh from which he rebelled—which he loved better than any place on earth?

When one asks oneself questions of this kind about most of the celebrated figures of the past—what would they think of their cities if they could revisit them to-day?—one has a fairly clear idea of the answer. They would be amazed, shocked, disgusted by this or delighted by that, each according to his character. They would always, however, be so confounded by the changes the years have wrought that they would scarcely recognize their surroundings. Doctor Johnson would not know where he was in the London of to-day. Even Dickens would be confused and perplexed, not only by physical changes but by deeper, more elusive transmutations in the huge city he once knew. Balzac would be lost in Paris; and the imagination does something more than boggle at the thought of what Metternich would say if he were to see Vienna. I think that when one considers Stevenson and Edinburgh one comes upon one of the rare exceptions to this general rule. R.L.S. would probably slide easily into the life of modern Edinburgh, and, after a few questions and adjustments, take his place there without difficulty. The reason for this is twofold. It lies partly in Stevenson's own feelings about Edinburgh and partly in the character of the city itself. R.L.S. loved everything young, lively and vital in the Edinburgh of his day. Were he to come alive now he would continue to do so. At the same time he savoured with a rich appreciation his city's rock-like immutability; he would still savour it to-day.

While it would be absurd to say that Edinburgh

is changeless it is, despite all that has been said about cinemas, the radio and aeroplanes, a city peculiarly little addicted or subject to change. Something in the deep core of London remains constant, but the surface of its life, visible, audible and sensible, shifts and moves like the sand-hills of the Sahara or the tides and waves of the sea. The great industrial centres in the course of a hundred years have grown bloated and confident, then decrepit or at least shabby and uneasy. The changes in Oxford are not confined to the obvious ones: they are subtle and profound. They would have come over that, at one time rather self-conscious home of conservatism, even if Lord Nuffield had never existed. Even the superb and frozen self-sufficiency of Aberdeen has suffered a literal or littoral sea change, with its beach pavilions and with the fact that it is becoming more and more a holiday resort. Many villages and small towns have remained unaffected by the years. But, save for Edinburgh, it is difficult to think of any large town which has not altered radically or superficially so much that a visitor from a hundred, seventy, perhaps fifty years ago would be quite confounded.

It is easy to account for this changelessness of Edinburgh by putting it down to the huge and almost indestructible physical things within her and immediately around her. Whatever you built on the top of the Castle Rock it would be difficult to obliterate its overwhelming presence in the centre of the city. You may turn the great houses of the

New Town into blocks of flats and offices, but, short of the inconceivable vandalism of pulling it down stone by stone (a considerable feat) you will not destroy that grand pattern for centuries. It would take an atomic bomb to change the shape of the shores of the Firth of Forth and something more than an atomic bomb to move the omnipresent Arthur's Seat or the Pentland Hills. Nothing that man has yet thought of could change the climate. And it is surely the climate, more than anything else, that is responsible for that odd quality of timelessness in the stone of this stony city—that quality that gives the impression in certain places and at certain times that the town has only yesterday been erected by a theatre-scene designer, and, at other times and places that it has always been there.

These physical things of rock, stone, sea, sky and air have their immediate effect upon the returning native. They convince him, as he emerges from his railway station at either end of Princes Street that everything is as it was; and he goes gaily forth confident of finding everything unchanged. It is only after a week or so of indeed finding everything unchanged that he pauses to ask whether this immutability is all a question of physical circumstances and whether there is not something equally important in the indigenous human element of the place. Gradually, if he stays more than a week or so, he becomes convinced that it is as important, and ends by thinking it more important. It is the people of Wigan and Paisley that make Wigan and Paisley, the people of Rome and Vienna that make and have made Rome and Vienna. The most important element in Edinburgh (with all deference to the guide books) is the people.

Robert Louis Stevenson was, as all who have read him know, profoundly influenced, from the beginning of his life to its end, by his native city and the people who lived in it. Its nobly dramatic scene, its vivid contrasts of splendour, order, decency and picturesque squalor, its louring past, its tantalizing contemporary present, its harsh yet at other times sweet surroundings haunted his imagination until, an exile in his last years, the memory of his city came to have the force of a dream that completely possessed him. Its people, too, would not let him go—the pawky, the romantic, the excessively respectable, the excessively disreputable, the abandoned, the dour, the douce, the young, the old, the vivid, highly individual characters of Edinburgh were with him in his mind until the end. And, what was perhaps more important, the sound of their voices was still in his ears and seemed to grow clearer.

He heard them so clearly in his last years, and his art has made them so audible to us, that they seem as real as the voices of Edinburgh to-day. It is, however, the Edinburgh of one hundred years ago, the year of his birth, that is our first concern.

CHAPTER II

THE last sedan chair disappeared from the streets of Edinburgh a year or two before Robert Lewis Balfour Stevenson (as he was christened) was born. This statement may be difficult to believe, but it is vouched for by the late Sir J. H. A. MacDonald, Lord Kingsburgh, Lord Justice Clerk. Kingsburgh may have been a pedantic, or arch writer, but he was obviously and laboriously truthful. He was born in 1836. When he says that sedan chairs were frequently to be seen in Edinburgh in his childhood, and before he was out of his "frocks", that would be about 1842, we may be sure that he was speaking the truth. We may be sure, also, that his infant eye did not perceive the last of them, and that one or two must have lingered on until nearly, or exactly 1850, when R.L.B.S. was born. Tradition supports this belief.

The fact that the sedan chair was in use in Edinburgh until half-way through the nineteenth century is very characteristic of Edinburgh. The fact that Stevenson was born just when it was disappearing, and lived just into the age of the internal combustion engine is very characteristic of Stevenson. For us Edinburgh people Stevenson seems, at times, to be the last of our truly eighteenth-century writers. At other times he seems to be the first (and still the first) of our moderns. Though Stevenson was certainly never carried in a sedan chair through the streets of Edinburgh, though he equally certainly never travelled these streets save in a hippomobile (a word that would have and may have delighted him), his short life bridges, not only in time but in spirit, the gulf between the chair and the car. In this very fact there is yet another link between Stevenson and his native city. Edinburgh must surely have been one of the last if not the last city in Europe to use the sedan chair. She received the invention of the motor-car simultaneously with the rest of the world. Yet the passing of the long lingering chair and the arrival of the now universal automobile made surprisingly little difference to the essential Edinburgh. The accident of the span of Stevenson's life between these two events is peculiarly appropriate in his relation to this immutable town.

Immutable, yes. Edinburgh, in its manners and way of life still is the most naturally eighteenth-century city in the United Kingdom. Still a hundred years cannot pass without making some changes, without sweeping things away as well as introducing new ones. Were the modern subject of King George VI, be he a citizen of Edinburgh or not, to be translated into the capital of Scotland a hundred years ago he would be surprised to find how much of the old Georgian era lingered on there deep into the reign of Victoria. It would not be the survival of the gracious things only that would surprise him—the noble architecture (it is still with us), the spacious way of life (Edinburgh is still the most spacious town in Britain), the formal manners (formality after a fashion is still preserved here), the antique civic customs (they are still kept up in a creaking way), and so on. No, it would be the cruder, more vital, less graceful yet virile, and in some ways admirable elements of the last century whose survival to so late a date would take him unawares.

Edinburgh in the eighteenth century was a city of high living, high thinking and high stinking. Her topers and trenchermen could drink and eat anyone from anywhere else in Europe under the table. Her brains set the intellectual fashion for the western world. Her drains and the smells of her streets were so offensive that they invoked the disgust of the by no means squeamish Dr. Johnson in 1773. And, in the same year, they inspired satirical verse from our truest Edinburgh poet, Robert Fergusson, who not only loved his own town but, from earliest years, must have been inured to her civic stenches. Today there remains with us a certain amount of the heritage of high thinking and a little, a very little, of the tradition of hard drinking. But of the old insanitary Scotch town and its vivid way of life there is small trace save in the shell of architecture. It is true that here and there a glimpse of half forgotten beauty, a waft of half forgotten rottenness will bring upon the senses a guff (an untranslatable Scots word) a guff from that dead world, stealing and giving odour. But like a guff it sighs and is gone.

In the year of Stevenson's birth this old Edinburgh was still living, only just living. Lord Cockburn's *Memorials of His Time*, that classic of late eighteenth- and early nineteenth-century recollection, had not yet been published and its author was to die as late as Stevenson's fifth year. The extraordinary merit of Cockburn's book is that it gives us an exact account of the Old Edinburgh, of the Old Town as recollected by and seen through the eyes of one who had joined in the move into the New Town, and who had seen the New World of the nineteenth century grow up around him. He had acquired the modern spectacles through which he looked at the curiosities of the past with modern vision, yet that vision (because of his remarkable memory and industry in taking notes) was exact and clear. This is a very different thing from, let us say, Boswell's fascinating Journals. In Boswell we see the eighteenth century through eighteenth-century observation. Lord Cockburn takes us back into the age of the Georges from well into Queen Victoria's reign. However remarkable and interesting this literary feat may be, we must not forget that Cockburn was there to do it, and though he lived to reasonable old age he was no Methuselah. He died at the age of seventy-five.

If Cockburn covered this span so easily we may be sure that there were many, many others who did so and lived even later than he did. When Stevenson was a child there must have been Edinburgh Judges of the Court of Session, lairds and even some of the nobility who could remember having lived in the Old Town before it was turned entirely into a romantic slum. It is true that they must have been the last of the old guard, even in their childhood. But with the odd capacity old people have for remembering far distant, rather than nearer things, they must have been able to recall something of the old life when duchesses, cobblers, lawyers, ministers and fishmongers all lived in swarming tall beehives of "lands" in the High Street of Edinburgh. Stevenson in his childhood must have seen some of those survivals. He may even have spoken with one or two of them.

The individual human survivors may have seemed, to contemporary eyes, to have stood out isolated like gaunt statues in the street amidst the swirling mob of change. We who look back at them from a hundred years, know that they were not so alone, so curious, such oddities as they appeared to those who actually saw them in their old age. There was far more remaining of the time of their childhood than either they or those who surrounded them then realized. Just as to-day there are many figures of Victorian Edinburgh still surviving, and just as they find in Edinburgh (if they would only recognize it) more remnants of Victorianism than they would anywhere else in the kingdom, so did Lord Cockburn and his coevals, unbeknown to themselves, continue to trail a good deal of the clouds of the eighteenth century about and behind them.

In 1850 the most aristocratic club in the town still served dinner in its coffee room late in the afternoon. Club dinners were not individual snacks, but communal feasts, and the set hour was between five and six p.m., the older members being sticklers for five. They sat, both the early diners and the late-comers of six o'clock, until nine or half past when there would be a general and nearly simultaneous rising. It was not until half past nine that the army of extra helps from the town would be summoned in to cope with the washing up of the dishes. This labour would not even begin until four or even five hours after the dinner had been served. I, who was born in 1901, remember an elderly relative telling me that as a young married woman she had been considered fast for putting back her dinner hour to seven o'clock. She tried to reassure her critics by saying that she was following the fashion of the Queen, who, it was reported, had been accustomed for many years to dine in Buckingham Palace at seven. Even this did not have much effect, for, it was argued, Edinburgh should be above aping London fashions.

Luncheon in this same aristocratic club (and though aristocratic in membership it was typical in its manners of upper middle-class life) was only luncheon and was not regarded as a meal. People just strolled in for a glass of sherry and a little light refreshment in the middle of the day. It was all that even their appetites could deal with after the enormous breakfasts they had taken and with the prospect of the more enormous dinners in the evening. Indeed many people did without the luncheon snack at all, considering it a frivolous interruption of the day's work, occupation or pleasure which took place between breakfast and dinner. Such a thing as afternoon tea, in purely masculine society, would have been an unheard-of piece of effeminacy. This rhythm of occupation and eating was of course eighteenth-century in its origin, and Edinburgh in its survival. It was not only my elderly relative's female friends who disdained London fashions in the regulation of their lives.

Drinking amongst the professional and well-to-do classes, though not so prodigious as in the previous century, was something in the same kind. It would be tedious to give statistics about the numbers of bottles consumed by single persons. It is enough to say that men sat down to drink early in the evening and did not stop until bedtime, taking easily and leisurely, over a period of hours, a quantity of wine and spirits that would amaze the jerky and erratic and spasmodic dipsomaniacs of to-day. Dram drinking amongst the well-to-do was despised as a weakness. Long and deep potations, with or without food, were considered an admirable habit of virility. Men no longer got habitually and incapably drunk every evening. But in a large number of houses they went straight from board to carriage or to bed. By this time, in 1850, the habit of joining the ladies upstairs after dinner was, in London, almost universal. It was far from universal in Edinburgh.

The true broad Scots, the language now described by the revived word Lallans, had completely dropped out amongst the gentry of Edinburgh. This is not to say that they did not know it. They could understand it, and on occasions speak it, as for instance, when a judge or lawyer wished to put a country or simple witness at his ease, or when a laird or nobleman wished to condescend (in the better sense of that much misused word) with his tenants or rural neighbours. Most of these people had heard the old Scots tongue from their nurses or the servants with whom they had been brought up. It was domestic and truly familiar to them. Many of them when surprised, or under the influence of deep emotion, might have used a word or two or even a sentence of the language easily, accurately and without affectation. In moments of supreme delight or in the agony of approaching death many must have found the old words wringing from them.

Southern education had not yet become so fashionable as to be a necessity for upper-class youths in the Lowlands and in Edinburgh. Nor had the imitation English public schools in Scotland begun to take a grip upon the more comfortable of the middle classes to the exclusion of such indigenous institutions as the Royal High School and the Edinburgh Academy. The Academy itself was much more genuinely Scottish then than it is now. The University was Scottish and Continental and not English, nor, as it is to-day, largely cosmopolitan. And while youth was as yet largely uncorrupted by the southern idiom of speech, the elder people clung proudly to their own Scotch way of talking and would have repelled the idea that they would have been in any way bettering themselves by speaking English like Englishmen. They had, it is true, turned their backs upon the true old Scots language, but they talked English like Scotsmen, and would talk about So-and-so having a strong English accent. Stevenson who came from a well-off family much addicted to travel in England and abroad spoke to the end of his days in what one of his latest Scottish Samoan friends called "an unmistakable Lothian voice".

The antipathy towards England was still strong, an odd survival, one cannot but think, of the antipathy against the Union of 1707—an antipathy which had been felt a hundred and fifty years before by men and women of all kinds, cutting through all divisions of class. That this feeling just before 1850 was by no means the sentiment of disgruntled or old-fashioned cranks is shown by the following speech made from the bench by a Scottish judge a year or so before Stevenson's birth. He was condemning some English mobsmen and their female accomplices who had been detected, upon their journey into Edinburgh, in the act of picking a pocket.

"Prisoners, you have been found guilty of robbing from the person. It is not often that I have to pass sentence on people of your description from England, but I hope that the circumstances of my being a Scottish judge will not be held to sway me in discharge of my duty. Yet I am not sure if the circumstances of your being English men and women is not a considerable aggravation of your crime. What did Scotland ever do to you that you should come here hundreds of miles to prey upon her unwary subjects? Was it not rather that you thought that her honest and simple people would become easy victims in hands made expert by the efforts to elude the grasp of English authorities?

Now the issue has proved that you made a wrong calculation not only as to the intelligence and sharpness of our people but as to the boldness and adroitness of our detectives. I hope that you will bear in mind, and tell your compeers in England, what we fear they have sometimes forgotten, that we have not renounced our emblem of the thistle—the pricks of which you may expect to feel when I now sentence you to sixty days hard labour—I am only sorry that I cannot make it a period more suited to your offence."

This fine sounding piece of almost eighteenth-century prose was, despite its obvious tone of bias, quoted with approval and gusto at the time. It was commented on with praise by the Edinburgh police and earned a place in a celebrated detective's memoirs. The judgment was, as I have said, delivered just before Stevenson's birth. I wonder if he ever saw it in the reprint of the memoirs. It would have delighted and amused him.

In the 1840's and 50's slum life all over the United Kingdom was villainous. It was, however, usually a fairly modern form of villainy—the product of industrialism. In Edinburgh there was not at that time much industrial development. Very few people in Edinburgh, as in Glasgow, Manchester and London, came in from the country lured by the prospect of high wages only to fester and grow rotten in the hovels built to receive them. Rather the inhabitants of the Edinburgh slums were indigenous, if not to the slums, to their environs and decayed within their own circumstances. And so it appears that Edinburgh slum life in 1850 came trailing clouds of putrescence from the previous century and not exhaling their own. If the lords and ladies had left the rookery of the Old Town completely by the middle of the nineteenth century the new inhabitants had always been there underground, or at least did not come from far. If a parallel is to be drawn from London it is rather that they reminded one of Hogarth's "gin lane" or Moll Flanders than of the drawings by Leech of low life in the pages of the oddly radical *Punch* of the 1850's.

The celebrated crimes of Burke and Hare, though they occured well on in the nineteenth century, have an antique flavour about their villainy. The unpleasant business of child stripping too recalls an earlier age. Bands of women would come down from the High Street and lie in wait for well-dressed children whom they could lure by the offer of sweets to side-streets. Here they would set upon them and strip them to leave them howling and naked in the Edinburgh blasts while the hawks made off with their spoils to the "fence shops" of the Old Town. While it is abominable to think of a frightened shivering child in any circumstances, one cannot resist a smile at the thought that future judges, advocates or ministers may, in their childhood, have stood yelling and stripped in the New Town of Edinburgh. If there is an echo of Moll Flanders and the early picaresque tales about this sort of thing, there is also a faint touch (difficult to define) of Jekyll and Hyde. All these and other curiously out-of-date evil things took place in the Edinburgh of 1850.

Ladies of pleasure abounded in the Old Town, and made their promenades in the wide thoroughfares of the New after dark. Some were appalling drabs. Others had a kind of gay vagrant impudence partly Scottish in kind and partly reminiscent of the lawless ladies of the *Beggar's Opera*. The same detective, in whose memoirs is included the speech of the Scottish judge quoted above, tells a tale of the sharpness of one of these girls. I cannot deny myself the pleasure of repeating it if (of necessity) condensing it here.

Jean was a Princes Street lass. That is to say, she was presentable and attractive enough to be able to display her charms upon the main street of the town without drawing undue attention to herself. She was perky, gamine and alluring. She had the reputation among the police of being light-fingered. They had a soft spot in their hearts for her, however, for she exercised her fingers within the pockets, for the most part, of the rather more disagreeable and snobbish of her clients. She was always complaining of the young gentlemen who would come out of the clubs by midnight, would talk to her, fondle her hands, and then make some excuse to be gone—thereby getting some kind of second-hand pleasure for nothing. The police, who were men as well as officials, had a contempt for this sort of thing.

One evening, a constable found her in altercation with one of these young men late at night and in Princes Street. The young man said that he had but engaged, or was engaged by her, in conversation, and that she had taken the opportunity to steal a five pound note from his pocket. He demanded that she should be searched. Difficult though it may be to believe, the constable did then search her in a superficial way even though it was in the public street. He did not find the note. "The young prig" as he was subsequently to be known was not satisfied.

"A woman of this kind," he protested, "has as many devices for hiding paper money as the devil has snares for the unwary." With which pious comparison he insisted that she should be taken to the police office and be more thoroughly searched. She was, and by a female officer. But there was no note found upon her. Her only money was two shillings and fourpence. "The young prig" was discomfited but not convinced. He was certain that he had had five pounds when he had begun to speak to Jean and that he had lost them before the constable had arrived. He could do nothing. But Jean could speak.

"An' whit aboot me?" she asked. "Wha' is tae pay me for my wastit time? I hae been here in this polis hoose o' yours for twa hours. In nae mair than that time I could hae earned twice five gowden guineas by my ain honest wark." She did not press her case however, but with a toss of her head at the police officer, and completely ignoring the young man who had been responsible for her arrest and the loss of her honest work, she went out into the early morning.

Two days later, in Rose Street, she came up to the constable who had arrested her. Seeking the quietest backwater in a street of many backwaters, she addressed him confidentially, and with an air of troubled seriousness.

She told him that she had been worrying about the incident of two nights earlier. She did not specifically admit to stealing the five pound note, but mentioned that she knew where she could put her hands on it. She added that she did not like to touch stolen money. The constable told her that she must lead him to the place where the money was hidden.

"Na, na," said Jean. "You would be for arresting me yince mair. Forbye, ye'd be giving it back tae yon young prig—and that I'll no permit."

The constable told her that he could give no guarantees as to what he would do, but gave her to understand that he was interested. Jean, perceiving this, hinted at a compromise.

"Gin I were tae gie ye a nod o' the head ye wad be able tae follow that nod in the right direction. Ye'll no be able tae arrest me then, but ye maun promise me ye'll no gie it back tae the young prig."

The constable repeated that he could not guarantee this, but was obviously weakening.

"Verra weel then," said Jean. "I'll gie ye the nod, but ye maunna follow it till I hae gone roon the corner intil Princes Street again."

By his silence the constable gave assent. Jean then began to finger the sleeves of his coat in an intimate and significant manner. She pointed out that the police had unusually large turn-ups to their sleeves. She continued in this strain while still touching his arm so that it seemed obvious to the constable that she was trying to restore the money. Then she said quickly.

"Dinna look in thae sleeves till I'm back in Princes Street. Walk on and wait till I'm gane."

Assuaging his conscience by the thought that he would return the money to its owner, the constable walked slowly on. Then he looked eagerly into the turn-ups of his sleeves. There was nothing there. He could not understand it. He could have sworn that he had felt her fingers deep in the sleeves. It was only a day or two later that he learned the truth in a public house where Jean had boasted of her achievement. She had hidden the five pound note in the constable's sleeve on the original evening when he had been searching her. He had, all unknowing, carried it about with him for two days.

Then, under the pretence of giving the money back by slipping it into his sleeve she had really abstracted it from him—thus, after a fashion stealing the same note twice over.

There is something very picaresque in the eighteenth-century manner of this incident—and not only picaresque but Scotch, or, at least Scottish or Irish. At any rate, if it is too much to say that it could have occurred only in Dublin or Edinburgh in the United Kingdom of that date, the story smacks of one or other of the two cities. It is again a story that would have appealed to R.L.S. Perhaps it did. It is a pity he did not use it.

The formally tolerated brothels or *bagnios*, patronized by Boswell and the eighteenth-century lawyers, had been suppressed. But, if the houses of ill fame in the vicinity of Leith and in the Old Town were scarcely official, they existed in 1850 much more plentifully than they do to-day. Places of rendezvous under the guise of private parties lasted well on into the century and advertised themselves by fairly open if ingenious methods. One monthly saturnalia took place in the upper room of a public house in Rose Street. The publican, having reached an agreement with a sufficient number of gentlemen, would fix the date. Then he sent a disreputable old piper round the streets and squares of the New Town. His arrival in such dignified surroundings as Moray Place or Heriot Row was the signal to the servant girls that the "party" was on that night. After midnight those who could beg, borrow or steal the keys of the area steps would slip out to meet the gentlemen in Rose Street. It is possible that, as a child, Stevenson may have heard, without realizing its significance, the sound of this disreputable missionary upon his rounds. Collette's establishment in *The Misadventures of John Nicholson*, though toned down in description, is obviously based upon some such Edinburgh "howff" of R.L.S.'s day. *Maisons Collette* still exist in the town of 1950. Their entertainment, however, is modified to the taste of this age, and is as watered as is modern whisky.

Whisky was the staple drink of all classes and almost the only drink of the poorer people. Gentlemen, of course, still took their wine; but the old claret days were over. Brandy, which had once figured in a poem by Robert Fergusson as the rival of whisky, had long been vanquished, and was nothing but an exotic or an expensive medicine. Beer, in the aristocratic club that has been already mentioned, was on tap free—for it was regarded as a drink not worth charging for and was not in favour in the poor man's pub at all. Whisky, and whisky alone was, as far as beverages went, solely responsible for enlivening, warming, inflaming or making rotten the mind of the nation and the capital at that time. By half way through the nineteenth century the public houses were officially closed at 11 p.m. in Edinburgh. But as they opened at six in the morning there was plenty of opportunity to indulge in whisky at twopence a nip or fourpence a glass and in its cheapest form at half a crown a bottle. The drunkenness of the working classes was savage and deplorable, but, in its way, it was cleaner than the hideous doping by means of methylated spirit and brasso essence which has taken its place in the great industrial centres of Scotland to-day. All classes, in their differing ways, drank more than now; and there was a general enfeeblement of physical health. But again, it is doubtful if there was any more secret drinking than now, any more dipsomaniacs, and any more people driven mad by the perverted use of alcohol than there are in 1950.

Indeed, certain public houses were made almost respectable by the fact that they were the headquarters of working men's clubs, whose purpose was not entirely that of conviviality, but almost of self-improvement, or at least of the search for knowledge This is illuminated by the fact that at the time of Stevenson's birth and for years after it (almost up till the time of the Education Act) there existed a character known as "the educated boy". The educated boy was usually a young man in his early twenties, who had acquired the ability to read, and read expressively, in an age when by no means all were literate, even in a big and cultured city like Edinburgh. The educated boy used to tour the various clubs in their various pubs with a copy of *The Scotsman* under his arm and a magnifying glass in his pocket. Even youthful eyes in those distant days found the print of *The Scotsman* too small for constant reading. The educated boy was charged not only with the task of reading the news, but of selecting the news. In certain clubs and pubs he would read only the political communiqués, in others he would read of literary or dramatic events, and of course there must have been clubs whose primary interest was sport. The whole proceeding was an odd precursor of the B.B.C. News Bulletin, and must have required a considerable knowledge of his audience on the part of the educated boy. It must also have required something more—a good hard head, for it was usual for the educated boy to be paid, if not in kindliness, in kind and in liquor at the end of his day.

It may seem excessive to dwell at this length upon the more savage, crude and Hyde-like element in the life of Edinburgh a century ago. I do not think so. Amidst the mass of literature written about Victorian Edinburgh there is an almost morbid avoidance of the subject. Memoirs abound in recollections of ladies' tea parties, church bazaars, solemn legal or civic meetings, opening with prayer and so on. To read them you would think that Edinburgh of last century really was like one of those sugary comedies, *Marigold* or *Lady from Edinburgh* which delight London audiences. It would be foolish to attempt to defend this crude, fleshly, not usually mentioned side of Edinburgh life of the period. It would be foolish to avoid notice of it, however, and idle to deny that it had a certain vividness and colour about it. It would be downright silly to pretend that it did not exist. I have chosen to speak of it at some length for three reasons. The first is that it is usually passed over in silence, and is therefore worthy of note. The second is that it was largely eighteenth-century in origin and character, and therefore germane to my argument. The third is that I claim that it played a considerable part in Stevenson's attitude towards his native city, indeed in his attitude towards life.

Of course there was the other and more notable side of Edinburgh life at the time. There was the great wave of religious feeling in the national church which led to "the Disruption" and the founding of the Free Kirk, with all the noble self-sacrifice, personal and general that that entailed. There was the self-denying passion of the Edinburgh scientists and doctors for research and discovery. There were the missionary endeavours and the genuinely liberal political movements. And it is not without significance that Edinburgh led the way (despite bitter opposition from within) to the emancipation of women in education. My own childhood, in the early years of the twentieth century, was spent in the family aura of the recollection of such things. We, as a unit in Edinburgh, took a civic pride in the memory of our city's proud record in such matters. It is therefore from no ignorance, from no distaste, nor from any lack of piety that I have not dwelt at length on the Dr. Jekyll side of mid- and late-Victorian Edinburgh. It is only that I take it largely "as read", because it has been written about so largely.

There was too, of course, the celebrated Edinburgh "pawky" character, full of pedantry or slow wisdom. He was to be found in both the Jekyll and the Hyde world of Edinburgh. He, too, has been so notably written about that he can be taken for granted.

The Edinburgh people of the mid-nineteenth century were probably more realistic than those who have sentimentalized about them in after years. They were well aware of the dichotomy in the character of their city. Indeed, they often saw and felt a similar dichotomy in themselves personally. Though they would not care to talk about it, they would not have denied it. I cannot think, however, that they worried much about it either in the city or in themselves. The psychological reason for this is that, whether religiously practising or not, they were profoundly influenced by Calvinism. Calvinism is to some of us a fundamentally detestable philosophy —the father of all determinism. It would be a mistake, however, to suppose that the Calvinist is necessarily a cruel man, or a harsh man, or one devoid of gusto in the many enjoyments of life. Indeed (once being saved) the very certainty of his position gives him a freedom in worldly pleasures denied to many who possess more uncertain but more troublesome consciences.

This is not to say that troublesome consciences did not exist in Edinburgh. To go back a hundred years earlier, we have the example of James Boswell. He was enisled in a sea of Calvinism in

Edinburgh, but differed from his surroundings in one fundamental fact. He had a conscience; it tormented him. There may have been other and less celebrated figures who were tormented by their consciences in the eighteenth century in Edinburgh; indeed, we are certain of it, though Boswell was the most celebrated. He was amongst the well-known figures of that well-known period, unique in respect of his conscience. Boswell's two favourite vices of drinking and wenching were far from uncommon in the Edinburgh of his period; they were, one might almost say, the prime relaxations of many of his associates. These relaxations did not, however, bother the consciences of his friends and his acquaintances. Boswell's conscience-stricken disgust at his own frailty was, amongst his circle, uncommon enough to be almost unique. His neighbours probably thought that his genuine fits of repentance were more funny than his pathetic vanity, certainly more funny than the lapses which always followed upon the heels of his repentance.

But even as long ago as Boswell's time, in the middle and latter half of the eighteenth century, strict Calvinism in the religious sense had been on the decline. Philosophically speaking, the frame of mind which it had produced could not be so easily thrown overboard. People did not say to themselves quite solemnly, "I am saved. Therefore I can do what I like. It won't make any difference." They did think something like this. "I am a respectable man. I go to the Kirk. I am a successful lawyer. I have bred a family to take on my estate. I cut a good figure. So what does it matter how I indulge myself?" If there lingered any element of religion or theology in their attitudes towards this, it would take the form of dismissing religious scruples about personal conduct as being Popish or Anglican. If pressed to defend themselves on this score (an unlikely contingency) they could probably have put up a fair, logical case based upon Calvinistic philosophy rather than on Calvinistic theology—if ever the old tag about the eighteenth century being the age of reason was true, it was true in Edinburgh of that period. Boswell, however, as we know, had strong and persistent leanings to a more humane and comprehensive form of the Christian faith than Calvinism. But it was not only his flirtations with, his hankerings after, or, as I would prefer to put it, his thirst for the Roman Catholic religion that induced his continual repentance. It was something deep in the nature of his soul and mind. For all his upbringing and his circumstances, he could never have adopted the Calvinist philosophy. He might have been a more contented man in this life if he had; but in eternity he will be sooner blissful for having been what he was.

If religious Calvinism had declined in the eighteenth century, it had grown even weaker halfway through the nineteenth, at the time when Stevenson was born; but its grip on men's minds and in consequence upon their behaviour, was nearly as strong as it had been a hundred years before. And it was this philosophy that was primarily responsible for the dichotomy in the mind and soul of Edinburgh to which I have referred. It was responsible for the Edinburgh of Hyde as well as the Edinburgh of Dr. Jekyll. It was, then, into this world, this strange, divided city that Stevenson was born exactly halfway through the last century.

His childhood, however, was spent under the influence of the most decent, humane and kindly form of Jekyllism—kirk going, missionary bazaars, and a quiet, loving and well-ordered home life combined with a decent, but liberal education. Later on he was to become aware of the presence of Hyde in his native city—perhaps to exaggerate it. But at the beginning all was sweetness and light, innocence, love and affection. This early period of his childhood and young boyhood was very vivid to Stevenson. It remained vivid in his memory all his life, quite as vivid as the Edinburgh of the times of his storm and stress, of his late adolescence and his youth. Together, or rather following one upon the other, these two periods of his life in Edinburgh went to make Stevenson the man and Stevenson the artist. It was these two periods, recollected in tranquillity, or if not in tranquillity in a state of nostalgia, that went to make the author of *Catriona* and *Weir of Hermiston*. It was the summoning up of this Edinburgh, two-sided in a way, yet unified in another, that stirred Stevenson to write his masterpieces from those "ultimate freshets" in the South Seas. There, removed in time and place, he was able to recall a picture of the city that was his birthplace, clear, vital and unified. It was a picture of Edinburgh in words which in clarity, vividness and artistry remains unsurpassed and has probably never been equalled in any writing about that city.

CHAPTER III

THERE is a common idea that men of genius or of artistic talent have usually been unhappy in childhood. This unhappiness is supposed to have created a loneliness of the spirit, to escape from which the youthful genius spins his tales or dreams his artistic dreams. However true this general supposition may or may not be, one thing is certain. It was not true of Stevenson. His infancy and childhood in Edinburgh were very happy. There is, it is true, a certain pathos in the ill-health and physical weakness of this extremely mentally active and imaginative child—a pathos made more poignant in the popular mind by the note of longing in the real charm of *A Child's Garden of Verses*. But that very weakness and ill-health provoked amongst those around him and those who loved him an extra tenderness and solicitude upon which his eager affection fed. There is no doubt about it—until adolescence or just after, Stevenson was very happy. He may not have made many friends amongst the children of his own age, but in his family circle he was never lonely, and, at first, his family was all in all to him.

He was the central figure in a pattern ideally created to make an imaginative highly sensitive child happy. It was a pattern which might later on have brought unhappiness and even permanent bitterness. In point of fact it brought, in later years, no more than some long periods of sadness, some deep misgivings and misunderstandings, all of which were in the end cleared up. It was a pattern which, though it may have been repeated after a fashion countless times elsewhere, was, as far as only children, or only boys are concerned, highly characteristic of the class in which Stevenson was born in Edinburgh. It was a very Scottish, a very Edinburgh pattern. Apart from the outer pattern of grandparents, aunts and friends of the family which undoubtedly influenced Stevenson's childhood, the central pattern was all-important. It was made up of three people. His father, mother, and his nurse Alison Cunningham. Each was equally important.

It has pleased those who insist that genius must somehow have been thwarted or oppressed in early youth in order to be genius, to portray the father, Thomas Stevenson, as a grim, inartistic tyrant, blind to the potential powers of his son, a religious bigot and a puritan. This view is particularly supported by foreign critics and those south of the Border. To them a mid-Victorian Presbyterian Edinburgh father of a brilliant boy must of necessity conform to this preconception. There's the label on the bottle; so what is in the bottle must agree with the label.

Thomas Stevenson was an Edinburgh upper-middle-class, well-to-do businessman. He was deeply religious and rigidly Presbyterian. He was conventional in his habits and notions. He was aloof and somewhat portentous in his speech. Though fairly well read, and with a proper respect for what he would call decent literature, he was not particularly devoted to the arts; but he was not without imagination. His two main interests in his life, apart from his family, to which he was deeply devoted, were his religion and his business as a lighthouse engineer. He had inherited his business from his own father; and he had much enlarged it. His religion was devout and was practised with humility. Some idea of his attitude of mind in this matter may be discovered in a letter he wrote which he directed should be read to a small group of his family and nearest friends after his death.

17 Heriot Row,
Edinburgh.

May I be allowed to say very humbly—God knows how humbly—that, believing in Christ, I confidently trust I shall not be disowned by Him when the last trumpet shall sound.

My good friends, I hope our friendship is not ended, but only for a time interrupted, and that we may all meet again in that better land which has been prepared for us by our Father and our Saviour, the blessed passport to which has been freely offered to us all. Amen.

Thomas Stevenson.

He himself really had been brought up in an atmosphere of hard, almost ruthless Presbyterianism. This had left upon his spirit the impress of a haunting unworthiness and melancholy. As I have said, he was not unimaginative. And it is possible that some part of his spirit was genuinely thwarted in youth. His imagination broke through now and again; and R.L.S. has recorded his pleasure in his father's conversation in these moods: "His whimsical fancies, his blended sternness and softness that was wholly Scottish."

He was essentially a kind man whose shyness often made it difficult for him to display his kindness. He must have been distressed by his son's youthful bohemianism of manner, dress and company. He must have been more than distressed when Louis professed a free-thinking creed near to atheism. And he must have been deeply wounded in another part when his only child flatly refused to enter the family profession to which he had succeeded, which he had built up, which many would have thought a romantic calling—the building of lighthouses all around Scotland. Still, he took all these distresses and disappointments very well. And, as far as the goods of this world are concerned, was generous to his son. I know the kind of man he was very well.

Apart from any hereditary powers that he may have transmitted to his son, his influence on him was important, and for the good. He provided just that amount of opposition which made R.L.S.

have to fight his way into the profession of letters instead of drifting into it—which he might well have done had he been left to the guardianship of his mother alone. He did incalculable service to the young Stevenson's mind in insisting that he should read for the Scottish Bar before he definitely set up his door plate as "Man of Letters". This discipline of mind was not only good in itself, it forced him to work hard at his leisure task of learning to write—for his leisure was now limited.

Thomas Stevenson was of the best of his kind and class in the Edinburgh of his time. His kind still exists. He was the best kind of father, in the immediate pattern around him, that R.L.S. could have had.

Stevenson's mother was again very characteristic of a kind of Victorian Edinburgh mother. Edinburgh women have been noted for their forthrightness of expression and sometimes for the dominance of their character. Many a nineteenth-century home in that city has been ruled by the puritanism, or at least, stern Presbyterianism of the matriarch. Such women have often been written about in memoirs and in fiction, possibly because they are picturesque or, at any rate, vivid in their kind. The other kind, of which Mrs. Thomas Stevenson was one, have not received the same attention. The Scottish word douce is the most apt to describe them.

Mrs. Stevenson had been brought up in a religious atmosphere, being a minister's daughter, but the atmosphere had been less hard, less Calvinistic, than that of her husband's childhood. She took her religion as naturally and as easily as she breathed, without melancholy or self-torturing misgivings, neither doubting nor constantly affirming. It was natural to her. Any possible remnants of manse severity (if they had ever existed) were softened and obliterated in her by the fact that God had been so obviously good to her. He had given her a husband whom she loved, a son whom she adored, and comfortable circumstances. She therefore thanked God all her life for His goodness and loved Him, not as a saint would love, but at a respectful distance.

This is not to say that she was a sheltered comfortable nonentity—far from it. She was buoyant, courageous (as is shown by her journey and the transplanting of herself late in life to Samoa) and had character. Her cheerfulness, her certainty that all was for the best, and that all would come out well in the end, influenced her more melancholy husband, who, it must be remembered, in that age of fine social distinctions, came from a slightly lower stratum in the infinite gradations of the mid-Victorian middle classes. It is certain that she eased the situation between father and son when it became difficult, not only because she loved the one and adored the other, but because she had sufficient strength of character to help each of the disputants to see the other's point of view.

Thomas Stevenson has sometimes been blamed

for not spotting early on that his son had a passion for literature which nothing could quench, and a talent, which, if allowed to grow, might become genius. It is easy to be wise after the event, and to elevate Mrs. Thomas Stevenson's belief in her son into an acute perception which her husband lacked. This is not so. Thomas Stevenson was probably a better literary critic than his wife. But Mrs. Stevenson knew their only child better than he did. She knew that his longing to be a man of letters was not ephemeral, but was radical in Robert Louis. She knew that if he was frustrated in this longing, his character would be fundamentally thwarted. So far, her support of her son was reasonable, or at least based on reason, if not exactly thought out. If, however, she saw signs of genius in the childish, adolescent, or early youthful literary products of her son, it was not because she had unusual gifts of criticism, but because she loved him—possibly the best reason for believing in anyone.

The third member of the domestic pattern immediately surrounding R.L.S. was a very familiar figure in the mid-Victorian Edinburgh household of comfortable circumstances—the unmarried, and otherwise unattached, but adoring female. Sometimes this figure is an aunt, an elder sister, a family friend, sometimes a servant. Alison Cunningham (the celebrated Cummy) was engaged as a nurse for Stevenson when he was eighteen months old. She remained looking after him in various ways until he was grown up. She stayed with the family until it was broken up by travels, marriages and deaths. After that she was pensioned off, to survive all other members of the pattern.

The servant who grows so familiar (in the best sense of that word) that he or she becomes a part of the family, is and has been a well-known figure in any part of the world where domestic service is not regarded as a despicable calling. He and she have appeared in countless memoirs, in innumerable volumes of fiction, and upon many stages. Scottish literature, factual and imaginative, is full of the type. This is because there is something in the Scottish character that makes the type particularly vivid, vivid in its dry or exasperating humour, vivid sometimes in its touching loyalty. The character too has survived more sturdily in Scotland than in many other places. Here is a quotation from Dean Ramsay's *Reminiscences of Scottish Life and Character*. The incident occurred just about the time of Stevenson's birth:

> "An old Mr. Erskine of Dun had a retainer under whose language and unreasonable assumption he had long groaned. He had almost determined to bear it no longer, when, crossing a field, the master exclaimed, 'There's a hare.' Andrew looked at the place and coolly replied, 'What a big lee, it's a cauff.' The master, quite angry now, plainly told the servant that they *must* part. But the tried servant of forty years, not dreaming of his dismissal, innocently asked,

'Ay sir, whaur are ye gaun? I'm sure ye're aye best at hame.' "

I myself at some period as late as half way between the two wars (about 1930) heard the following dialogue between a Judge of the Court of Session in Edinburgh and his manservant:

Master: I think I'll walk to the station. It's a fine evening.

Servant: It's no a fine evening.

Master: All the same I prefer to walk.

Servant: Ye'll dae no such thing, my lord. I'll call ye a cab.

Master: I tell you, James, I want to walk.

Servant: Dinna be so headstrong, my lord. Ye'll no walk while I'm here to fetch a cab for you. It's rank foolishness for the like of you walking on a night the like of this. Ye're getting an auld man. I'll no let ye walk, my lord, and that's that.

Master: Oh, very well, then.

The extreme familiarity of the old Scottish servant is not (as some have superficially supposed) rooted in the democratic tradition of "a man's a man for a' that", or "Jack is as good as his master". The true Scottish domestic would repel such an idea, if anyone had the hardihood to put it to him. No, the familiarity springs from a deep sense of possessiveness. The family belongs just as much to the servant as the servant to the family. Sometimes this possessiveness discovers itself, as I have said, in exasperating bossiness, sometimes in touching loyalty, but possessiveness is at the root of it all.

Alison Cunningham had this domestic possessiveness developed to a high degree. Naturally, it was focused for the most part upon the baby, the child, the youth and the young man who was her first care. But there are signs that she was inclined to possess Mrs. Stevenson too. She probably saw only the portentous, the shy, the melancholy side of Thomas Stevenson, her master, and made no effort to include him in her possession. In any dispute within the pattern of the family, her by no means insignificant aid would be given to "her laddie" and her mistress first. As her mistress was usually inclined to understand, if not always to approve of what "her laddie" did, there was not likely to be any clash between the two women.

I have put the words "her laddie" in quotation marks because it was as "my laddie" that she referred to him to the end of her days. It says a good deal for the sweetness of Mrs. Stevenson's character that she appears to have shown no resentment when Cummy, after R.L.S.'s death, and in Mrs. Stevenson's presence, would show her treasures of early photographs and signed editions to visitors to a running accompaniment of remarks such as—"This is my laddie when he was first out of frocks." "This is my laddie when they cut his hair short when I was away." "This is the first book my laddie gave me," and so on. The only half-smiling protest which Mrs. Stevenson made was to her son, when public reference after reference was made to the nurse who had soothed the author's feverish hours in infancy. She pointed out that she had spent quite as much time as Cummy had in the sick child's bedroom, doing the same as Cummy. R.L.S. made the not very convincing reply that a mother's devotion was taken for granted, while Cummy's services were bought, and, the services being exceptional, demanded exceptional recognition.

At any rate Robert Louis was "her laddie". By the time he had reached adolescence and young manhood, she regarded herself as in possession. With the loyalty of the old Scottish servant, combined with the woman's capacity for not seeing what she did not want to see, he could, in her eyes, do no wrong. Short of his committing public and open blasphemy or becoming a Roman Catholic, she would have supported him against all attack, all criticism, even from his father. At the back of all this highly feminine, this highly Scottish domestic loyalty was Alison Cunningham's deep and inbred Calvinism. If she had not been taught the purest and most rigid doctrines of sixteenth-century predestination, something of the quality of those doctrines had lingered on to be absorbed by her in her childhood in the remote Fife village of Torryburn. I do not think that she would, if pressed upon the point, have admitted for one moment that any baby upon birth was predestined to eternal torment, but she certainly believed that some souls were "saved". Of these saved souls, it is quite certain that she believed "her laddie" to be one.

It was Cummy rather than his father or mother who first implanted in Robert Louis' childish mind the passionate devotion to the Covenanting cause which was in varying degrees, and in differing ways, to remain with him all his life. As a child, the Covenanters were saints of the purest kind to him, and the persecutors the blackest devils. As he grew older, and had passed through various stages of disbelief and belief, he modified his view of the Covenanters' absolute rectitude and the absolute villainy of their opponents. But always the memory of them tugged at his heart; and in his celebrated poem to S. R. Crockett, about his "Hills of Home", the plain words, "the graves of the martyrs" stand out as starkly and as noticeably in his verse as do grave stones upon the heather-coloured hillside in autumn.

As to how far Cummy passed on to him at second hand, as it were, the inbred Calvinism of the doctrine of salvation, which she felt rather than reasonably believed, it is impossible to do more than guess. She had a profound influence upon this highly sensitive and mentally acquisitive child, and it is difficult to think that she cannot have implanted in him some notions of his certain salvation. These may have subconsciously remained with him during his bohemian and free-thinking days, and may, without him knowing anything about it, have given him a certain delicious freedom in playing with what was supposed to be sin—the freedom of the Calvinist who knows that he cannot be damned. It is impossible to tell: one can only idly speculate.

There are odd rumours still current about that mysterious business of "Kate Drummond", the blacksmith's daughter at Swanston with whom R.L.S. had an affair, and who is said to have borne him a child. Rumour still says that it was Cummy who was the principal figure in routing, or at least dealing with, the girl's indignant father. It may have been (on rather stronger evidence than rumour) Thomas Stevenson who forbade R.L.S. to carry out his emotional or chivalrous intention of marrying the mysterious Kate. But rumour still has it that behind, enforcing, perhaps overpowering this parental command, there was Cummy who refused to allow "her laddie" to be dragged down by such low creatures into a disastrous marriage. She may have been wounded and distressed by his frailty in allowing himself to be mixed up in such a business, but *he* was not to suffer for it. No, it was the evil people who had tempted "her laddie", her saved one, who should be punished. The rumour may have no basis in fact, or it may be an exaggeration. But it certainly is in character.

It is tempting to think (as some have suggested) that we should know more about this episode in Stevenson's youthful Edinburgh days if he had lived to finish *Weir of Hermiston*. There is no doubt about it that though disguised in appearance, manner and in many other little ways, Kirsty is based upon Cummy. The heroine of the story, though made dark in hair (possibly to please the author's wife), is almost certainly the blacksmith's daughter—or whoever the mysterious "low love" in Edinburgh was. Archie Weir is R.L.S. as a young man almost undisguised. The situation, before death interrupted the book, was working up to one not unlike that which it is generally supposed R.L.S. found himself in, over his first love affair.

I do not think, however, that we should have learned much about the facts of Stevenson's early affair had *Weir of Hermiston* been finished. Stevenson's art had advanced far beyond mere autobiography in his masterpiece. He was drawing upon his own experiences only in so far as they helped him to create a story outside himself. Moreover, so ingeniously had he spun this story that he had made Kirsty's loyalty divisible—that is between her adored young master and her niece, her own flesh and blood. Finally Stevenson, by the time he was writing *Weir of Hermiston*, had long ago escaped from the influence of the harsher side of Calvinism which was no more a part of the fibre of his being than it was of the unhappy James Boswell's. He would have shrunk from portraying such a creed at its crudest, when he remembered, and from a great distance, only the more picturesque elements of those who supported it. He would have shrunk from such an act especially if the portrayal had had some roots in an experience in his own past youth in Edinburgh or Swanston.

Alison Cunningham was a woman of very strong personality. It has long been the fashion to "debunk" such characters some thirty or forty years after their death. Let me assure the reader I am indulging in no such odious practice. The Cummy cult at its height (during the period between Stevenson's death and her own) may be a trifle embarrassing to look back upon, but it was hardly the poor woman's fault. If fault there be, it was Stevenson who started it all off with his dedications, his printed tributes, his letters and the like; but even then it was a fault of judgment arising from genuine love and affection and nothing else. And it must be remembered that even when he was at his most famous, R.L.S. could hardly have foreseen what his admirers would do with the Cummy cult, let alone the R.L.S. cult after his death. If he had, he might have been more restrained—but then again he might not. Affection and love are difficult emotions to curb. Cummy was in R.L.S.'s mind, ineradicably linked with Edinburgh when he was separated for ever by half the earth's surface from his native city. Why should he restrain the public expression of homesickness when that homesickness was, in a sense, personified in a distant and still living person?

No, in a country and a century responsible for producing a number of remarkable women, Alison

Cunningham was in her own humble kind remarkable. She was a Scotswoman who, under her handsome appearance, and in her brave and devoted character, had many of the faults and most of the virtues of her race and country thick upon her. I, for one, not only respect, but admire and like her all the more for it.

If, in this book upon R.L.S. and his city, I have dwelt at some length upon the well-known facts about the pattern of his immediate family surroundings, it is because I believe it is apposite to my theme. Of course, in countless other cities and towns, in many other countries, you could have found, and may still find brilliant, eager, emotional only sons; shy, portentous, melancholy, excessively religious fathers, longing to understand but never quite managing to understand their children; sweet-tempered, loving mothers acting as affectionate links between the two; and, at the back of all three, possessive, devoted, religious females imported from without the family circle. It is a human pattern, which is, I suppose, a part of European civilization. Nevertheless I repeat what I implied at the beginning of this chapter. There was, in the way this pattern displayed itself in the family which Thomas Stevenson founded, something particularly characteristic of the Edinburgh of R. L. Stevenson's class and time. It is difficult, without going into laborious and boring detail, to define what I mean. Any Edinburgh-born person over thirty years old, coming from Stevenson's class and condition (which are also mine) will know what I mean.

The pattern or family of Stevenson began in a small neat house in Howard Place on the most northerly fringe of Edinburgh's gracious New Town. Within half a dozen years Thomas Stevenson's affairs had so prospered that he and his family were able to move more towards the centre of the city, up into the spacious surroundings of Heriot Row—still one of the most commodious as well as one of the most beautiful streets in Edinburgh.

Though Stevenson's earliest memories were of Howard Place, it was in Heriot Row that he came properly to the full consciousness of his surroundings. In that ample house—to-day it would be regarded as too large for a family of three—looking south into whatever sunshine reaches Edinburgh, with its long, wide gardens in front of it, with the Castle showing itself in proud glimpses at the corners of the intersecting streets, and Princes Street only a few hundred yards up the way, R.L.S. must have realized the fact of Edinburgh for the first time.

It was from his nursery window in Heriot Row, he tells us, that he watched through sleepless nights the glimmer of a light in a window in Queen Street away across the gardens. He used to wonder whether this meant that there was another feverish unsleeping child in that distant house—probably it was some advocate sitting late over his briefs. It was from the Heriot Row windows that he used to watch for the lamplighter on his nightly rounds, and longed to join him in his (what seemed to the child) romantic noctambulations of the city. Heriot Row Gardens are amongst the largest and most varied of their kind in Edinburgh. They are surrounded by forbidding railings, and only the householders of Heriot Row or Queen Street have the keys of entry. They are still wonderful places for children who are lucky enough to have the right to play in them. In Stevenson's early days they must have been ideal for a child of his imagination. They must have seemed the size of a prairie and full of infinite variety of winding paths, well-kept bushes, shrubs and flowers.

Then out at Colinton, only three or four miles away, there was the manse garden of his maternal grandfather. Here was a smaller but equally entrancing wonderland of his own, or at least of his own family's, with the high woods hanging over it, and the as yet unpolluted water of Leith running at its foot. Behind the river, and above the woods, there rose the Pentland Hills, which to the child Robert Lewis must have seemed prodigious mountains. Later on he was to live at Swanston in the foothills of the Pentlands themselves and grow to love them as he would love no hills or mountains anywhere else in the world. As a child they were remote and romantic to him. For it was upon these hills, and in their folds, valleys and glens, so Cummy had told him, that the martyrs of the Covenant assembled to worship God in their own way at the peril of their lives. When the summer day's play in the manse garden was over, he would ride back in the carriage and, from Craiglockhart, see all Edinburgh stretched before him. The Castle and the Old Town with its plume of smoke drifting would rise from the centre of it. Arthur's Seat, lion-like, and Salisbury Crags precipitous to the east of it would seem as tremendous as the Pentlands that he had left behind. To the north, the Forth, silver or blue, would wind its widening way to the sea.

The daguerreotype which is produced as the frontispiece to this book gives a happy impression of R.L.S. at this stage of his life. The long, sensitive face, the fine eyes, the partly sulky, partly humorous, boyishly sensual mouth, that no later moustaches could quite conceal, are all there and are familiar to us. There is even present in the picture the habit of consciously posing which he was to display perhaps a little extravagantly in later portraits. The pose, however, is a happy and, so to speak, a natural one. He is the "young master" at the farm, riding his donkey in fine style, while the farm laddie, his squire, (one hesitates to call him Sancho Panza) stands behind respectfully but, unfortunately from the point of view of the daguerreotype, not immobile.

This picture came my way in an odd fashion. I had been staying last year, near Lasswade at the foothills of the Pentlands. An old man, who had passed all his days in that part of the world and who was then in his ninety-fifth year, heard that I was writing a book on R.L.S. for his Centenary. He asked whether I would be interested in a photograph of the boy Stevenson, which he had in his attic, and which he thought had never been seen before. I was most interested. The old man informed me that the Stevenson family used to come out for occasional holidays to stay at the farm next to that in which he (my old friend) had been brought up. On one occasion a daguerreotype photographer had also been staying at the farm and had taken a picture of Stevenson with the young son of the farmer. This young son, who was exactly the same age as R.L.S., and who would now be a hundred, had died well before the end of last century. Before doing so, however, he had given to his neighbour this daguerreotype, asking him whether he would care to keep it. The daguerreotype then proceeded to lie in the darkness of an attic for fifty years, until it was produced for my inspection. Had it not been so treated, it would have faded long ago. It is now fading, but fading only slowly, beneath cloth covers in the Stevenson Museum in Edinburgh.

There can be no doubt, from what he said afterwards in conversation, from what he wrote in his letters, and from the scenes that he inserted into his books, that the romantic appeal of his native city seized him in early childhood. If final proof is needed it is to be found in *A Child's Garden of Verses*. These poems, though written in retrospect and in manhood, reflect the unmistakable quality of a child's mind. There are some who find the poems sickly and embarrassing. I cannot agree. They are so intensely evocative not only of a child's feelings, but of an Edinburgh child's feelings, that for me at least any affectations of style, any slight hint here and there of a deliberate attempt to catch the unconscious simplicity of childhood are swept aside and forgotten by the poignant emotion that they truly express.

The physical harshness of Edinburgh in certain moods struck him early in his life. The east winds tormented his already weak throat and lungs. The winters seemed interminable, the springs intolerably delayed, and capricious when they arrived. He had, however, early opportunity of contrasting Edinburgh's greyness and her buffeting weather with the other and softer scenes. Quite soon in his childhood he was taken on account of his health on visits to England and to the South of France. Later on he was to be almost as much devoted to France as he was to Scotland. But as a child, despite the physical ameliorations of those southern journeys, Edinburgh came easily first in his affections.

It was not only because of the romantic appeal of the city which his precocious imagination had already partly perceived, it was because Edinburgh was home to him. And his home, from its inner circles to its outermost rings, was intensely happy. Everyone was kind to him. There were no jarring notes. He had not yet learned either to disagree with his father nor to fear his disapproval. Thomas Stevenson, too, found it easy to be natural with the gay, eager child whom he had fathered. He had not yet acquired the portentous shyness in the family circle which he was later on to use to protect himself from the alarmingly heterodox and bohemian youth which his son was to become.

His mother, Cummy, and the manse circle out at Colinton lapped him round with love, affection and care. He breathed this in as easily as a normal person breathes air, and, surprising though it may seem, does not seem to have been spoilt by it. He even absorbed their piety, and invested it with a kind of gusto. He wrote childish essays upon Biblical themes, and in his early adolescence had printed (at his father's expense) a history of the Pentland Rising—the first fruits of Cummy's early indoctrination of the Covenanting theology. This little paper pamphlet was produced to be sold at a Missionary Bazaar which Mrs. Stevenson had organized at her house.

A Missionary Bazaar! All the comfortable, decently pious atmosphere of 17 Heriot Row, Edinburgh, is in that phrase. Mrs. Stevenson presides at her table in the big drawing-room. On the table are laid the various objects contributed by the family, the friends, and other members of St. Stephen's congregation. They are to be offered for sale in support of the Church of Scotland's missionary funds. These range from tea cosies, bedroom slippers, work boxes, and other Victorian articles of domestic use, to Benares jars and other Indian gewgaws brought back by returning missionaries from the fields of their labours. The table, so we learn long afterwards, held goods in sum total up to and over the value of seventy pounds. Fairly, but not too prominently displayed, is a pile of pamphlets offered at fourpence each. They are by the son of the house, who mixes eagerly but a little nervously with the crowd. He is anxious to see how his first printed work is going and to know what people think of it. It sells pretty well, for Mrs. Stevenson is popular and people like to please her. Moreover, her boy's eagerness, politely suppressed, but none the less obvious, is rather appealing. He does not, however, have much chance of hearing criticism of his booklet. He is only a boy; and people think it sufficient to praise him warmly and genuinely for having been able to write it at all.

The writing, printing and sale of Robert Louis Stevenson's *The Pentland Rising* occurred just about at the end of his boyish days in Edinburgh. The Missionary Bazaar at 17 Heriot Row is a fitting scene on which to ring down the curtain on that happy, eager, innocent period of R.L.S.'s life. Though he was shortly to see another and different side of Edinburgh life, this early period laid the foundations of his attitude towards his native city.

CHAPTER IV

The curtain that fell upon the pleasant domestic piety of the scene at the Missionary Bazaar at 17 Heriot Row was shortly to rise and show us the young Robert Louis Stevenson in a very different setting in his native city of Edinburgh.

The Victorian drawing-room is replaced by the public houses and pawnbrokers' shops of Leith Street, Rose Street and the Old Town. The occupant of the bedroom from which the child used to watch "Leerie" the lamplighter is often not in bed by midnight now. For, after eleven o'clock, when normal places of entertainment close, he knows where to go. There are "howffs" round by the Calton Hill which cater for those who wish to sup and drink and enjoy themselves in other ways until deep into the early hours of morning. There are the rooms of the richer and more independent students where young men may entertain ladies and drink whisky or wine and talk heterodoxy until the dawn. And, most exciting of all, there are "thieves' kitchens" and "seamen's haunts", vague and hidden resorts in Leith and in the street that leads down to it. Only the pallid light of an Edinburgh morning or the occasional intrusion of the police can break up these gatherings so fascinating to watch from the fringe, so tempting in their dangerous defiance of all the conventions of the Jekyll side of nineteenth-century Edinburgh.

The appearance and manner too of the eager boy who had been the author of the pious pamphlet *The Pentland Rising* has undergone a startling change. The boy Stevenson had always been out of the ordinary to look at, even when he was neatly dressed and carefully groomed. He was angular, awkward and jerky in his movements. Only the expression in his fine eyes, the obviously vivid intelligence of his long sensitive face had saved him from being almost ridiculous. As a boy he had had easy, uninhibited manners (some called them French) and a gaiety of demeanour which had made him, at children's or young people's parties in Edinburgh, as conspicuous as a kingfisher would be amongst a gathering of starlings.

Now, in his secondary Edinburgh period, his oddities are exaggerated by farouche clothing, long hair and other peculiarities of dress, toilet and behaviour. Finally, as if to confirm the worst fears of those who love him, to express in words the inner horrors of which these clothes, this way of life are but the outward and visible signs, he speaks of his scorn for contemporary Edinburgh morality and crowns it all by announcing himself a disbeliever in the creed of his fathers.

"Oh fine religious decent folk
In virtues flaunting gold and scarlet,
I sneer between two puffs of smoke,
Give me the publican and harlot."

If he does not quite dare to display these juvenile verses within the family circle, he certainly allows himself to express in less picturesque words the sentiments they enshrine. The decent upper middle-class society of Edinburgh to which his parents belong begins to shun him openly in Princes Street and George Street. There is genuine and deep sorrow in 17 Heriot Row. Only the family love, loyalty and affection, the devotion of the mother, the imperturbability of "Cummy" and the truly Christian tolerance of the awkward, shy, distressed father prevents there being a major domestic disaster.

Immediately after the 1914-18 war (that is to say by the time that the death of Mrs. R. L. Stevenson and all other parties who might be offended had made speculation and research safe) there was a spate of writing about this "bohemian period" of R.L.S.'s life. This was inevitable. In the early 1920's Stevenson was enjoying a second wind of popularity, especially in the United States. He was an obvious subject for that truffle-nosed industry at which American scholars are so adept. Moreover, this period in his life, this element in his composition as a man and an artist had been so obviously, so heavy-handedly, so firmly suppressed by the official and semi-official biographers and reminiscencers that it was asking too much of human nature to expect it to refrain from investigation into the forbidden territory.

Some of this investigation and exposition was

not only inevitable; it was necessary and was well performed. Mr. George Hellman in New York, who stumbled upon evidence on this subject almost by accident, by acquiring a number of Stevenson's early unpublished poems, was first in the field. His many researches into the writings on the officially suppressed side of Stevenson's life were animated by a sincere desire for the truth, and, equally important, by an affection and admiration for R.L.S. the man and writer. While he was rightly angered by the existence of the "Stevenson myth", so sedulously propagated by his early biographers, he was less concerned with what many writers might have regarded as the agreeable task of exploding that myth than with presenting a true and likeable portrait of the subject of that myth. There is very little, if any, of the glee of the debunker in his essays and writings on Stevenson, and a very good deal of scholarship and human feeling.

Unfortunately most of those who followed Mr. Hellman in writing about R.L.S.'s "bohemian days" lacked either his ability or his single-mindedness of purpose or both. There is about their essays, their "imaginative reconstructions" and the like, an unpleasant air of half-shocked, half-tittering salacity or, incredible though it may sound, of sentimentality quite as bad as, and, in some instances, worse than mawkishness of those who were responsible for the "plaster saint" of the Stevenson myth. This again, was perhaps inevitable. If a writer of genius has been, for over thirty years, held up to youth as the example of purity and good behaviour, if he is extolled for having kept his pen out of the inkpot of *fin-de-siècle* decadence, if he is continually being referred to as "healthy in his outlook", small wonder if the fastidious are apt to turn away from the example so laboriously set before them. Small wonder, if, when the truth is discovered, the prurient and the salaciously sentimental rush in to enjoy themselves, to surprise the fastidious, and to shock the idolaters. One may not have much taste for the productions of these people's minds, but, human nature being what it is, one can hardly blame them. No, the blame rests with those who, in the first instance, concealed the truth, erected a false image, created an unhealthy action and an equally unhealthy reaction.

It would be outside the scope of this small book to argue in detail, or indeed at all, the rival merits of the cases put forward by the idolaters and the "debunkers". Apart from anything else, the task would be unnecessary. Most of the verifiable facts about this period of R.L.S.'s life have been discovered and discussed; but at this distance in time we can view them dispassionately.

I do, however, intend later on to examine Stevenson's "bohemianism" in so far as it is relevant to my theme—R.L.S. and Edinburgh. But before going on to those chapters, it is more than I can do to resist ending this one by making some reflections on the mass of misconceptions that arose about this unfortunate youth's time of *Sturm und Drang* for many years after his death. Unfortunate, I mean, in regard to his treatment at the hands of those who have written about him.

The first mistake was one that the mythologists were eager to make. They claimed that this phase was trivial and unimportant. The second mistake, made, equally eagerly by the inquisitive (let us say rather than the iconoclasts), was to exaggerate its importance beyond all measure.

The mythologists, who began their labours fairly soon after the death of their subject, would have liked, one suspects, to have passed over in silence the "Velvet Coat" period of his Edinburgh days. This, however, was impossible. There were far too many people in that city of long lives and long memories, who could remember looking down their noses at "young Stevenson's idiotic cantrips", who could recall that they shunned him in public places, who may even have expressed their sympathy with Thomas Stevenson in the distress he suffered on account of his erring son's ways. No, the period had to be mentioned and accounted for somehow. And so it was decided that Stevenson's early and vivid rebellion against the conventions and the most cherished beliefs of his class, kind and time, was only a rather silly phase attributable to a youthful vanity which, at a safe distance, could be mildly, half-laughingly rebuked, and, in the light of the fruits of subsequently displayed genius, forgiven. "It was only youthful high spirits and soon over," they say. Though whether they would have so indulgently excused the same "youthful high spirits" in another son of Edinburgh who had not turned out to be a world-famous writer, is doubtful.

The anti-mythologists, the enemies of the idea of the plaster saint (be they animated by iconoclasm or only inquisitiveness) go to the opposite extreme. They are right in pointing out that Stevenson's "bohemianism" was more than a passing phase, that a taste for it remained with him all his life. But they are far too insistent on it. They leap with glee upon his comparison of himself with the Edinburgh poet Robert Fergusson—"weak, vicious and tormented"—and harp upon the carelessly uttered epithet "vicious" as if it were a confession of all sorts of secret wickednesses. Above all they exaggerate to an absurd extent what they conceive to be Stevenson's outrageous peculiarities of behaviour at this period of his life. To read some of the strictures upon poor, unhappy, romantic "Velvet Coat" you would think that no other writers and artists in the latter half of the nineteenth century had behaved oddly, indulged in poses or dressed to attract attention. Shades of Wilde, Beardsley, Baudelaire, Whistler, Yeats!

The truth is, of course, that Stevenson was not only behaving in a way in which many other young artists and writers had behaved before him (and since), he was being positively normal. At the time in which Stevenson grew up to the perception of the world around him, the romantic spirit of the age was expressing itself in what was then known as *La nostalgie de la boue*. It may be easy to smile at this form of romanticism now, but it was probably just as easy at that time to smile at Wordsworth's discovery of mountains, valleys and lakes. The honey that ran, mixed with the mud in the gutters of Paris, London, Vienna and even Edinburgh, was infinitely alluring to the young artists of Western Europe who had been taught to taste of these artistic and literary pleasures by Baudelaire, Swinburne and the rest of them. Stevenson was avid in his reading of French and English poetry in the 1870's, and when he was just emerging into manhood. It is not at all surprising that he fell under the influence of these verbal enchanters. It would have been astonishing if he had not. He was, in fact, undergoing the ordinary and normal experience of a literary-minded young man of the late nineteenth century. Unlike a number of his literary contemporaries, he had the courage, or at least the vitality to pursue his nostalgia for mud beyond poetic exercises and to translate it into fact. In Edinburgh too, he had a particularly suitable background against which to put his theories into practice.

In this fact lies part of the trouble, part of the reason why the "Velvet Coat" legend had persisted to the detriment of R.L.S.'s memory. Part of the gusto displayed by the debunkers may be due to their pleasure in exploding a legend built up by the idolaters, the mythologists, the Plaster Sanctifiers. Another part of that gusto arises from the fact that they are able to indulge their own rather tinsel sense of the dramatic by displaying the "Bohemian Stevenson" against the background of "Puritan Edinburgh". One can well understand that such a contrast may have seemed irresistible to superficial and posthumous biographers. There, in fact, they were completely in the wrong. There can have been few cities in Europe, let alone the British Isles, where the *nostalgie* for *boue* could have been more easily indulged in than in Edinburgh of the nineteenth century. It was not the fact that the young Stevenson found and trod the not very hidden path to the Edinburgh Avernus that aroused the comments of his contemporaries. It was, as I hope to show in my next chapters, the manner in which he haunted it and lingered in it that caused them to talk. It was his honesty and romanticism about it all that surprised them and even shocked them. It is the faint and distant echo of that surprise and that shock that one hears in the dying but still spasmodically current rumours and legends of "Velvet Coat" in Edinburgh.

CHAPTER V

By the time that Stevenson was making his first bohemian explorations of Edinburgh, that is about 1870, the last outward remnants of the eighteenth century had been swallowed up in Victorianism. The picturesque remnants which I referred to in an earlier chapter as lingering on till the year of R.L.S.'s birth had gone. The sedan chair of 1850 had found its final resting place in the museum. Lord Cockburn had been dead for sixteen years; and with him, or just after him had disappeared the last of those who could, even by a fantastic stretch of memory, recall the final glories of the Old Town. Knee breeches and wigs, which in Edinburgh had survived longer than anywhere else in the United Kingdom, had vanished so completely that they had not even the shelter of museum to preserve them. Fancy waistcoats were on the decline; and whiskers, beards, and drab grey clothes for men had come in. Edinburgh, though never a city of commerce, was prospering indirectly as the capital of a small country whose trade in the west and elsewhere was expanding vigorously. There may have been no millionaires, but the comfortable classes in the city were more comfortable and more numerous than they had ever been before.

Outwardly the eighteenth century had gone, but it lingered on even now in the manners and mannerisms of the people just as, in the faintest possible way it lingers to-day. The fashionable world still, as in 1850, dined fairly early, even by Victorian standards. Edinburgh old ladies still allowed themselves a forthrightness, a downrightness of speech which was a direct inheritance from the Duchess of Gordon, Lady Grisell Baillie, Mrs. Patrick Cockburn and other matriarchs of the High Street, in the previous century. Elderly relatives of mine used to allege that swearing, amongst these old ladies, had not quite gone out by the 'seventies. I am inclined to think that this was a picturesque exaggeration. Even I, however, can remember from my childhood, just before the first World War, the truly obliterating powers of rebuke possessed by some of the older female rulers of Edinburgh society. Its devastating effect needed no reinforcement of oaths. It was complete in itself. In the 'seventies men of middle age in Edinburgh still preferred snuffing tobacco to smoking it. Wine drinking, as opposed to whisky tippling, was, even amongst the comfortable classes, on the decline, but it existed as a custom after something of the old fashion in quiet corners and in private houses. The railways had now firmly joined Scotland and Edinburgh to England and London, but the quickness of transport had not obliterated from the minds of the Southern Scottish aristocracy that Edinburgh was their capital—

something more than their county town. I have said that the Scottish accent was, in 1850, universal in the capital. Twenty years later the first emigrant wave of youth towards an English education had begun amongst the well-off classes in Edinburgh. That uneasy and uncomfortable hybrid, the Scottish Public School based on English models, had been established. Amongst the more snobbish then of the younger people, the English voice was becoming fashionable. But the Scottish accent, the Scottish way of using the English tongue was far from being despised (as is, alas! too often the case now) with the middle-aged and elderly. Not only ministers and lawyers, but Scottish peers of the realm, Scottish lairds in and around Edinburgh spoke, if not Scots, Scottishly and never dreamed of being ashamed of it. They were probably more native in their speech than was the London-loving Boswell and quite as Edinburgh as David Hume.

But perhaps the strongest link that remained with eighteenth-century Edinburgh was to be found in the eccentrics who continued to flourish there. Eccentrics have always been the capital distinction of small capital cities. This distinction remains with Edinburgh and Dublin even to this day. In both cities they have provided an unbroken succession of type originating in the eighteenth century and passing vividly right through the nineteenth. It may be that, in old and self-contained small cities and ancient foundations, such as the capital of Ireland and the capital of Scotland, the eccentric has been encouraged to linger on account of conservative tradition. It is equally possible that the strong sense of individual personality that marks the inhabitants of these and similar cities has been responsible. In societies where everyone is positively expected to be himself or herself, and not an imitation of somebody else, eccentricity of behaviour and thought flourishes easily.

The eccentrics of the Edinburgh of 1870, as in the previous century, and, as to a certain extent, nowadays, were of very varying kinds. Some were pawky, or pious, or otherwise peculiar in the accepted "Scotch" fashion. Others were flamboyant in clothes, speech and parade of learning. Some were wild and dissipated, seasoning their periodical debauches and disappearances into the underworld with a kind of extravagant distinction or even with long bouts of drunken pedantry. These and other oddities had only one trait in common—none of them was young. Some of them were middle-aged; the rest of them were elderly. It was a curious fact, which R.L.S. was to discover to his own discomfort, that while Edinburgh would tolerate almost any peculiarity of style or behaviour in a man of over forty, it was profoundly suspicious of eccentricity in youth. That was "bohemian", foreign, and not Scottish.

Eccentricities—those like deep drinking, running after loose women were all habits that could be allowed to the established and the middle-aged in a quite prosaic fashion. They must not, however, be romanticized. Young men, as the wiseacres of mid-Victorian Edinburgh knew, were inclined to invest their irregularities with a specious romance, even to sentimentalize them. This was not approved of. Professor Blackie might parade Princes Street in his peculiar plaid and his straw hat; elderly advocates might enjoy their interludes from Presbyterian morality at regular intervals in as startling a manner as they chose; old-fashioned journalists, men of letters and servants might affect any peculiarity of dress and behaviour that seemed suitable to them; even ministers of the Kirk might grow their hair to a prodigious length, showing off their fine profiles, and might indulge in rhetorical speech and extravagant gesture. All these were allowable, and were, within reason, to be smiled upon and encouraged: they were a part of the old Edinburgh. It was not, however, permitted for the young men of the city to imitate their elders in such matters. If they did they brought an excess of feeling into irregularity of conduct which was uncomfortable for the general civic body. It was in such an atmosphere, against such a background that the young Robert Louis Stevenson began his own career of eccentricity and bohemianism. All Edinburgh, both the conventional and the permittedly unconventional, were naturally opposed to him. It was only in the true underworld, amongst the unselfconsciously unconventional, that R.L.S. of the velvet coat was accepted without question.

The underworld of the Edinburgh of 1870 had its sharp and clear geographical limits. It began in certain streets within a space of scarcely more than a few yards, and ended as abruptly. Apart from the areas given to its larger habitations it emerged in odd little islands right in the heart of the city's most prosperous and respectable quarters. The close juxtaposition of wealth and poverty, decency and squalor, rectitude and laxity, had been a quality of Edinburgh's that had endured for centuries. Not even the great eighteenth-century break with the past, the building of the New Town, could obliterate it. The grandees who designed the splendid plan of Princes Street, George Street, Queen Street, Moray Place and so on, may have thought that, in turning their backs upon the Old Town, they had expelled squalor from their midst, or at least left it behind. They reckoned without the poor who, particularly in Edinburgh, were always with them. Even to-day these close and oddly foreign juxtapositions, these islands of squalor and laxity in the midst of wealthy respectability, still exist. Perhaps the outlines of division are not so startling and clear as they were eighty years ago, but they are faintly romantic and exciting even half-way through the twentieth century.

It is not to be wondered at, then, that the scarcely more than adolescent R.L.S. found these contrasts and juxtapositions of varying ways of life exciting and romantic in the Edinburgh of his day. Chesterton has pointed out, and others have remarked how much Stevenson was attracted by sharp outlines and clear contrasts. In his descriptions of scenes, even in his accounts of men's faces and bodies, we see what he lays before us as if he had cut it out of paper with sharp scissors. There are few or no dim edges in Stevenson's imagination as he displays it to us in his fiction. This clarity of outline is increased by an effect of style of which he was very fond. He will cut and hack his way through carefully balanced sentences at appropriate moments with beautifully appropriate monosyllables giving, again, a knife-like edge to what would otherwise be luxuriant verbiage. This quality in Stevenson's mind, though shown in his writing and his use of his imagination, was no acquired writer's mannerism. It was, one cannot help feeling as one reads the accounts of his childhood, born in him. It displayed itself triumphantly in his first successful piece of fiction *Treasure Island*. It is supreme in his unfinished masterpiece *Weir of Hermiston*. How the contrasts of Edinburgh must have appealed to him when he was eighteen or nineteen—that is when he was old enough to be allowed to notice and explore them.

There were other reasons why he should be drawn to the immediately near underworld of Victorian Edinburgh. He was in a rebellious frame of mind. He was rebelling not so much against his parents and his home, but against the society of which they were a part, and the beliefs which they unthinkingly (it seemed to him) held. Here was a world of natural rebellion against his own order, lying just at his own doorstep. But it was not only its convenience that attracted him. It was exciting to be able to wander at ease and with freedom in an outlaw world that was just round the corner from law, order and comfort—much more exciting than going to London or to Paris. The rebellion was all the more piquant for being carried on within a few minutes' walk from the noble rectitude of Heriot Row, and within the confines of the reputedly douce and respectable Edinburgh. Any youth who is inclined to romanticize low life feels that the low life that is near to his respectable life (and therefore dangerous because of its proximity) is more exciting than remote low life.

Then there was the passion or the fashion for *la nostalgie de la boue* to which I have already referred, which was prevalent amongst most of the *avant garde* of the young artists and writers in Western Europe at the time of R.L.S.'s youth. I have already pointed out that Stevenson, with his early acquired and easy knowledge of French, with his restlessly romantic temperament, would have been prone wherever he was placed, to have fallen under the influence of this particular mood of the *Zeitgeist*. It must be added that, if he needed any further encouragement, it was provided by the fact that his youth was spent in Edinburgh. The tradition of Edinburgh low life has always been that it should be vivid. It still is in a somewhat reduced manner. This vividness is not due to any affectation or to artistic posturing amongst its inhabitants as in Paris or in other Continental cities. It is natural, and is a direct legacy from the days of Deacon Brodie (a character that fascinated Stevenson) and the days of the Old Town on the Castle Hill. This very vividness, as well as its ready proximity, made it a bold and exciting step to explore it. You cannot now, and you certainly could not in Victorian days, go into it without feeling the influence of its vividness upon you. You could not, as could a Parisian aesthetic youth, make sporadic darts into your local low life and emerge feeling untouched by it. Whether you were horrified by Edinburgh low life or were subtly attracted by it, it had its effect upon you. To enjoy *la nostalgie de la boue* in Edinburgh was, for a young man eighty years ago, to make a very defiant gesture—however romantically that gesture may have been conceived. All this must have added to R.L.S.'s natural and Scotch predilection for a French fashion.

Finally, it must be repeated that, at a time when nearly all the Edinburgh of Stevenson's own class was either condemning him as a wanton hothead, or laughing at him as a foolish young poseur, it must have been an immense relief to have found a society, almost at his own doorstep, that accepted him without question and without mockery. His companions in the "howffs" around the Calton Hill, in Leith, or in the Old Town may not have understood one word of his poetry, still less of his deliberately cultivated poetic and romantic attitude towards them, they may have thought his velvet coat peculiar, his long periods of shy silence incomprehensible; and they may have been at a loss (should anyone have asked them) to account for his presence amongst them, but they had one great compensating virtue. They did not question him. They may have laughed at him, but they did so in a friendly way. All these oddities of his which the rest of Edinburgh was so quick to condemn as a kind of personal insult to itself were in the underworld *his own affair* just as their own often more illegal and sometimes criminal oddities were *their* own affair. This tolerance of human differences in human society is the assuaging quality of the underworld, wherever it is to be found. It has assuaged many an artist other than Stevenson who has found that his own natural world cannot thole him any more than he can thole it.

It requires an effort of the imagination to call up the feeling of the underworld of mid-Victorian Edinburgh, but, the effort having been made, it is, for one who knows the city well, who has lived in it since childhood, not difficult to reconstruct. The effort is necessary because Edinburgh, in common with all other cities in the United Kingdom, has long abolished most of the outward and visible signs (as regards permissible human conduct) of the old underworld. Places of entertainment, places of drinking, even of eating, in short all casual resorts have had, since 1914, to be subject to rules and regulations which, if they have not converted them all to complete respectability, have made them easy to supervise by the police and by all kinds of societies interested in public morality. Nowadays it is only necessary for the police or the interested society to prove that the owner of a place of public resort has broken some trivial rule about time, to have the licence of that owner taken away. The police and these others have the right of entry to examine that these regulations are being kept. The business of catering to public refreshment or public entertainment is now open to such constant inspection that it is difficult for any genuinely irregular conduct to take place.

This was not so eighty years ago. The police marked off certain areas of any great town (and particularly of Edinburgh where the contrasts of living were so great) where they knew irregular and illegal things, such as the meetings of thieves or the keeping of houses of ill fame, were taking place. Having decided that certain habits of human beings in large societies such as towns were impossible to suppress, they, the authorities, thought it as well to permit these habits provided that they were confined to certain districts where they need not offend the well-to-do and the respectable. There was, too, for the authorities a certain advantage in this segregation of the disreputable and the irregular. When things became too warm, or when a serious criminal was on the run, the police knew the geography of the underworld and were able to move in it with ease. It was a cynical, possibly "realistic" view of crime and irregular behaviour which would shock our reformed society today. But after all it is doubtful which society would shock the other more, could each have seen the other —ours or that of the middle of Queen Victoria's reign.

Very little of the old underworld of the big cities in the United Kingdom now remains. It has been abolished, driven even further underground, or dissipated. At any rate it is not visible to the casual eye; and any visitor from the middle of the last century would presume, from a superficial inspection, that it has been entirely wiped out. He would see poverty, squalor in certain places, and might even remark a peculiar kind of bedragglement of look more general in this age than in his. Of the old vividness, the old shamelessness of the underworld, he would see nothing. If, however, this visitor out of the past were to come from mid-nineteenth-century Edinburgh to mid-twentieth-century Edinburgh, he would at least see something that would remind him of the low life of the old days—the architecture.

In nearly all big cities in England, and to a lesser degree, in Scotland, the actual habitations of the Victorian underworld have been or are in process of being pulled down. At any rate they are so physically changed as to be almost unrecognizable when one compares them even with the old faded brown photographs. A ghost from the last century would not know his way about.

But he would in Edinburgh. As façades, if not entirely as interiors, Leith Street, and its purlieus, the High Street of the Old Town and its tributary wynds and closes, Rose Street (between Princes Street and George Street) and other squalid intersections into the midst of the still prosperous and dignified New Town, still remain almost untouched. This is due partly to the immense solidity of some of these buildings, partly to the natural conservatism of the small capital of Scotland which, compared with other towns, has not expanded much in a hundred years, and partly, let it be admitted, to the fact that some of these remnants, such as the major portion of the Old Town, have acquired the almost inviolable status of being "picturesque quarters". At any rate they are still there.

This, then, is the first reason why, having made the mental effort to visualize the past, it is not too difficult to reconstruct the scene of the nineteenth-century Edinburgh underworld even at this date. The shell remains. But then, as a second reason, and as anyone sensitive to the feeling of Edinburgh knows, there remains something more than the shell. The old quarters of old cities, provided that they have not been irreparably improved by town planners, retain a kind of smell that is more potent upon the imagination even than upon the nose.

This sounds not only platitudinous but sentimental. It produces recollections and visions of well-meaning American and British tourists wandering around the old parts of Avignon and Carcassonne eagerly snuffing up what they suppose to be the last enchantments of the Middle Ages, when they are really only smelling open drains and garlic. In order to make it quite clear that I have not this kind of amiable sentimentality about the old quarters of Edinburgh in mind, let me say this.

I do not believe that, in the genuinely Old Town of Edinburgh on the Castle Hill, it is possible for any but historical experts to extract any atmosphere or suggestion of the pre-Reformation or Reformation period. And even such suggestions and faint atmosphere as may be detected by the trained eye and nose are built upon small and often hidden pieces of indiscriminately scattered pieces of architecture. Even the eighteenth century, the great period of the High Street, the Lawnmarket and the Canongate, does not really discover itself to the visitor to-day—and this despite the fact that much of the building has been allowed only to decay and has not been structurally altered. No, it is that very decay of these celebrated streets of the Royal Mile that makes its most forcible impact upon the eye and the imagination not only of the visitor, but of the Edinburgh citizen. There is no one particular century that is obviously triumphant here. It requires, if not expert knowledge, at least an historic rather than a sentimental sense of the past, some reading, a knowledge of Edinburgh as a whole, and possibly a quiet Sunday afternoon when the long straggling street is deserted, before anyone can really begin to visualize what it must have looked and felt like two hundred years ago. There are, however, streets and quarters of Edinburgh that really do carry the atmosphere (even for the sluggish imagination) of a past which may not be as remote as the eighteenth century, but which is nearly as extinguished. And though, it is quite true that the eighteenth century to-day lingers more in Edinburgh than in any other city in the United Kingdom, it is a faint and far-off thing. The underworld of the middle of the last century is nearly as faint. But it is not quite as faint. You can feel its lingering ghost in certain places in the city; and you do not need any book-learning to perceive it.

Here is only one street to illustrate what I mean, but it is an apt one for my purpose. At the end of the famous Princes Street full of comfortably rich if ugly shops, and with its superb and compensating prospect of the Castle and the Old Town, the thoroughfare in one direction seems to peter out into what is merely a direct route out of the city. In the other direction inclining and declining to the left it slinks off by way of Leith Street and under the shadow of the Calton Hill into Leith Walk and thus to the port of Leith a mile or so away. This inclination and declension that comes so abruptly at the end of one of the most opulent as well as one of the most celebrated streets in Europe became, shortly after the New Town of Edinburgh was well and truly laid, a real descent

to Avernus for Edinburgh youth and all who
wished to escape (whatever their age) from the
wealth and respectability of the Scottish capital.
Christopher North placed his partly imaginary,
partly factual *Noctes Ambrosianae* in a "howff"
just at the head of Leith Walk. But these rather
turgid symposiums were the most respectable
meetings ever to have been recorded in the district
from 1820 for a century onwards. And by the time
that the last *Noctes* was going to press, North may
have been wishing that he had been able to change
the venue of his now famous gatherings to a part
of Edinburgh less notably associated with the
primrose path. The heady fumes of the underworld must have been rising round "the Blue
Parlour" in the inn in West Register Street fairly
thickly by the 1840's. The fumes are not so palpable,
so sensible, nor so visible nowadays. Indeed they
are but a faint mist apparent only to the sense of
the imagination. But, granted that faculty at all,
they do make themselves felt. I defy anyone who
possesses it not to perceive it as he swings leftwards
and downwards from Princes Street into Leith
Street.

How can one define the feeling that quite
certainly takes hold of one at this place? One
cannot. One can but point here and there to
elusive outward and visible forms of the impression
that one is receiving inwardly. First, there is the
fact that, leaving the wide openness of Princes
Street, one is plunging into a canyon of suddenly

enclosing, fairly high houses. There is the simple business of going down a curving hill after the propriety of walking straightly and on the level. Then there is, for the Edinburgh-born man, or, at least the inhabitant of Edinburgh, the knowledge that he is taking the first steps to leave the reputedly austere and withdrawn capital of Scotland and is on his way to the sea, to the ships and the port of Leith where (only by repute) a different morality obtains. But there is something more. There is an indefinable air of crapulousness about the façades of the fine early-nineteenth-century houses. The upper pavement on the left-hand side of the street which, in an oddly Continental fashion, runs over the tops of the swarming little shops (thereby relieving the main and lower pavement the pedestrian traffic so suddenly congested after leaving the amplitude of Princes Street), seems raffish rather than dignified. You can see slum children who have emerged from hidden staircases in the back streets playing and squabbling on the safety of this elevated highway. Above the children, who are above you, swing the signs of pawnbrokers and old clothes merchants. Upon your own level, in the lower street, the public houses grow more frequent and more crudely alluring. The echo of the tram-cars and the lorries in the valley whose sides rise round you upon your descent, grows clamorous and insistent after the steady sussuration and monotonous murmur of Princes Street. Foreign names begin to appear upon the shop fronts. All these shops are obviously respectable, but you will catch glimpses, in the byways leading off and declining from this declension, of more dubious establishments—entirely legal, of course, but offering the protection of some kind of umbrage to their customers who might not care to be seen entering their doors from a crowded thoroughfare. The nervousness of these customers must be supposed to be acute. None of them would be in danger of meeting their maiden aunts in Leith Street, though they may have left that possibility a bare two hundred yards behind them away up there in Princes Street. And accompanying all this visible and describable decrepitude there is the intangible sense that somewhere close behind these high façades there are backways, wynds, small places and lanes from whence have emerged these careless and perambulating crowds. They cannot have come from Princes Street.

If this be the impression given by Leith Walk halfway through the twentieth century when the quarter has been supposed to have been "cleaned up" for more than thirty years, it may be imagined what it must have been like in the 1870's when Stevenson first began to explore it.

"It was like a guff," a man once said to me, who was old enough to have enjoyed exploring this quarter of Edinburgh as a youth in the early 'eighties. "It was like a guff of life when you passed the Register House and left the clean air behind you." (The contempt with which he used

the word "clean" cannot be conveyed in print)—
"and smelt the cigar smoke and the whisky and the
patchouli coming up at you in waves."

"Cigar smoke?" I asked him, for that was hardly
the kind of smell that, even in my earliest days, I
had associated with this not very luxurious part
of my native city.

"Ay, cigar smoke," he repeated. "In those days
we all smoked cigars, sailors, students, bookies,
young men and old men on the loose of all kinds
and classes. Cigarettes! Man! People didn't know
what a cigarette looked like in 1880; and you'd
have been laughed at for a jessie if you'd smoked
one in a Leith Street pub."

I too, as I talked recently to this old man, could
remember that I had in my youth caught whiffs
of this "guff of life" as I had escaped from Princes
Street into the downward and Leithward path.
Though by that time—it was in the 1920's—the
guff had become considerably fainter than in my
old friend's day. Still, as he used the vivid phrase,
the sense of it came back to the nostrils of my memory.
Some of us who were undergraduates immediately
after the 1914-18 war, turned back quite deliberately
to the fashions of thirty years before in the 'nineties,
as a reaction from the disagreeable present—as it
then seemed to us. *La nostalgie de la boue* was
enjoying a kind of second wind amongst certain
of the youth of my generation. In my early twenties,
I was, if nothing more, certainly not ignorant of
the look, the sound, the smell, and to a limited

extent the argot and customs of the underworld of many towns other than Edinburgh. Yet, upon my homecomings to my own city, the swing from Princes Street into the Leith descent always seemed to me just as exciting, sometimes more so, than similar explorations in southern and foreign cities.

Was it only that, like Stevenson, whose background and whose inclinations had been not unlike my own, I was enjoying the piquancy of contrast between the profound respectability of the town of my childhood, as I remembered it, and the crude vividness of its underworld so recently discovered? Was I exaggerating its vividness and its crudity just because it was discovering itself to me in Edinburgh? This element may have entered into it, but it was, I am sure, far from being all the reason for my romantic excitement in this and other similar quarters of Edinburgh.

No, the Leith descent, with its glaring lights, and particularly its more shaded and obscure environs had, even as late as the early 1920's, a kind of directness, a shamelessness of appeal which could not be accounted for simply on the score of contrast. Within a few minutes, within the space of a few hundred yards, all the century-and-a-half-old Scotch reserve seemed to be obliterated from people's faces and from their speech. Things were much less wrapped up here than in even the lowest quarters of London and elsewhere. They may have been expressed less gracefully and with less superficial allurement, but they were there for you honestly, crudely and vividly. Here was a world in which anyone might talk to anyone and say what he wanted in a public house, without having to have the excuse of drunkenness. The veneer was off. It is true, of course, that there were laws and regulations. There was little if no violence. Places had to close on time; but there was always a back room, a back door, or a way round. While, as for the rather dreary, but would-be daring all-night resorts that remained open till the morning, my English friends, whom I used occasionally to take upon tours of them, were frankly taken aback and sometimes a little alarmed by them.

"I didn't know such things were allowed in England," they would sometimes say.

"This isn't England."

"I mean Britain, of course," they would correct themselves.

"This isn't Britain. It's Scotland, and Scotland's old and wicked capital at that."

There would be a pause, then one of them would ask, genuinely for information, "I say, is this place a café or a dance-hall or a witches' coven?"

"As you please," I would say. "As you please."

As they pleased! Whether they pleased or not, I was, I am sure, even though I did not know it at the time, enjoying something of the allure that had drawn R.L.S. to these Avernian fields of our native city. "Something" is, of course, the operative word; for the circumstances of Avernus had been much reduced between my youth-time and Stevenson's. Even had I been conscious of the past, which I was not, I could have caught no more than a reflection of what he had seen. Still, it was a reflection; and I did, all unknowingly, catch it. In recollection I know this. To quote Stevenson from a very different context, "My heart remembers how."

What were these and similar parts of Edinburgh like during the period of Stevenson's youth when he visited them? The old man's phrase about the guff of life coming up Leith Street and Leith Walk gives one a hint of it, but only a hint. There were in the 'seventies no dance-halls or all-night cafés of the modern kind. Men went to their pleasures more directly then, and did not need the excuse or the aphrodisiac of "the jigging" to go to it. Cinemas and popular opiates of the kind were, of course, unknown. There was only one music-hall-cum-theatre; though sing-songs of a fairly free nature used to take place in pubs and in semi-licensed halls. There were a few side shows after the nature of our modern pin-table saloons and a fair or two. But pleasure was mostly confined to drinking, singing, midnight gatherings for carousal and of course venery. Ladies of the town, amateur as well as professional, abounded; for the East of Scotland people have always been highly physically amorous. Not only were the streets thronged with those seeking and selling bodily pleasure, but there were houses of ill fame which advertised their purpose quite openly.

In every respect the contrast between the two worlds of Edinburgh was then much more sharp than it is to-day: it was also much more openly admitted. The difference was not merely between wealth and poverty; it was the difference existing between two societies enclosed traditionally in a small and ancient city—two societies living contiguously but with completely different values. It would be too much to say that these two Edinburgh worlds tolerated each other, but they certainly took very little notice of each other, and, as compared with to-day, scarcely interfered with each other at all. They were, in an odd kind of way, at once too close together in Edinburgh and too far apart for either to be able to afford to pay much heed to the other.

The inhabitants of the New Town and the richer suburbs, whether aristocratic or "professional", went their daily and evening rounds of work, pleasure and social exercise, without even having to think of the kind of life their less fortunate, but in many ways freer, fellow citizens were living just beside them. They might look up at the picturesque heights of the Old Town and reflect that much of their country's history had been enacted upon that strip of rock, but they seldom allowed themselves to think of the kind of present history that was going on there in the swarming "lands" while they looked at it. If they did not consider the life of the historic part of their city above them, still less did they allow themselves to know about the less "romantic" quarter that lay below them—the even more disreputable descent to the sea from the East End of

Princes Street. And, all the time, what made this sharp contrast of the two worlds so distinctive, so different from the contrasts of the two kinds of life in London, or even Glasgow, was that all this was packed into so dramatically small a space. Within the small and traditional enclosure of the capital of Scotland these two highly traditional Scottish worlds lived together, pretending to be unconscious of each other, yet sharply aware of the dividing line between each other.

It may well be understood that no respectable woman ventured eastwards and northwards of the Register House in Princes Street unaccompanied. Even if in masculine and protective company she would only go in a cab and under the compulsion of having to visit Leith in order to take ship from there. Indeed, there would scarcely be any other reason for her to visit Leith. That unjustly suspect adjunct to Edinburgh—for at that date it had scarcely become a suburb—had suffered from the reputation of the approaches from Edinburgh, and what was once a respectable township on its own fell under a cloud. I have heard, in my childhood, of an old lady who asked an extremely respectable-looking cook for her references.

"I was with a lady in Leith . . ." began the cook.

"There are no ladies in Leith," was the reply.

Despite this malodorous reputation, however, despite the presence of the ladies of the pavements and the houses of ill fame, despite the crude and unashamed atmosphere of these districts, the Leith descent, its environs and other similar parts of Edinburgh were not really villainous or dangerous. No, on the whole, the Edinburgh underworld, as regards law-breaking, cruelty and general brutality compared rather favourably with the underworld of nearly all other big cities in the United Kingdom. Edinburgh had been almost untouched by the industrialism which had bred the worst evils in Glasgow, Manchester, Liverpool and London.

This is not to say that these evils did not exist in the Edinburgh of eighty and a hundred years ago. They did exist, and they did display themselves from time to time as the fascinating police-court records and police-detective memoirs show. But it was not these evils, the existence of genuine vice and real brutality and undoubted law-breaking that gave the underworld of Edinburgh its reputation at that time. Two factors contributed to that reputation. The first was the contrast between the lower and the upper world of Edinburgh. The second was the colour of the life and the vividness of this forbidden world in this east-coast and ancient capital of Scotland. These are qualities that are highly suspect by, even repugnant to, the respectable in any age—and particularly in the age during which Stevenson was a young man.

However, be that as it may, it was to this half brightly lit, highly coloured, half-hidden and twi-lit part of his native city that the youthful R.L.S. fled for solace and for his dreaming during his period of uncertainty and stress.

CHAPTER VI

I MAKE small apology for trying to set in some detail the scene of Stevenson's youthful revolt in the underworld of his city. This period of his life, as I have said earlier, has been much misrepresented. Those who really knew the Edinburgh of R.L.S.'s young days have, for the most part, in what they have written about him, remained silent, or have taken refuge in vague generalizations. Those who, thirty or so years later, discovered something of the truth, or what they believed to have been the truth about Stevenson's "suppressed years" have worked under many disadvantages at the time they wrote.

They were at a distance in years. There was little written evidence for them to use. Those who could remember, and who could give them information, were evasive or silent or, which was just as bad, inclined to exaggerate from boastful or salacious motives. But their greatest disadvantage was that, being American or English, they did not know Edinburgh. They had no idea of the atmosphere of Stevenson's city, the atmosphere which was existing when they wrote and (as I have tried to make clear) lingers even till to-day. Atmosphere is a vague and much misused word, but the idea which it expresses is important when one is trying to write about the Edinburgh of Stevenson's twenties and his attitude towards it. These later writers were certainly industrious. They dug up a number of facts, but the facts were disconnected, and could not be seen in proper proportion without a feeling for, as well as a knowledge of, Edinburgh. Lacking this, they often made the mistake of thinking of R.L.S.'s revolt as if it had occurred in one of their own home towns, or, worse still, saw it against a preconceived and popular notion of the capital of Scotland which was quite false. As far as I know no Edinburgh writer of recent years has attempted to view the youth of Stevenson against the Edinburgh of his youthful and stormy days.

Still less am I inclined to apologize for what I am about to do, and that is to try to recall what R.L.S. actually did upon these explorations of his into the shadow world of Edinburgh of the late 'sixties and early 'seventies, to assess what was his attitude towards it. This period of his life was formative and important. I am as impatient with those who dismiss it as a passing phase of protracted adolescence as I am with those who exaggerate it in an attempt "*pour épater les bourgeois*". I admit that any attempt to get at the truth in this matter, to steer an accurate and dispassionate course between these two mistaken extremes, is primarily a business of feeling. One must feel for the facts which, sparse though they may be, are still scattered here and there. One must feel also *with* Stevenson. One must sympathize with him in the true sense of that word. How are the known and unconnected facts about this period of his life to be woven into one reasonable and psychologically satisfying pattern? Only thus—only by the proper use of credible hearsay, by an objective examination of the allusions in his writing and by an intelligent sympathy with his attitude towards life as a young man in Edinburgh.

The known facts about Stevenson's escape from Heriot Row into the other world of Edinburgh are few and simple, but revealing. The places to which he fled are as follows. The Old Town, the islands of disreputability intercessing the New Town, and the descent to Leith and its environs. I cannot find that he got much pleasure of the homesickness-for-mud kind in his researches into the Old Town. It was a part of the city that may have been (in the mood he found himself at the time) a trifle too obvious for his subtle, youthful and inquisitive mind. It was already becoming picturesque and tourist-haunted, even at that date. Moreover, it was a part of the town associated with the University. And R.L.S. was never happy while attached there. It was not so much that he feared the touch of the authority of his pastors and masters in that district, it was only that he was a little apprehensive that he might meet some of his fellow-students. In the islands of squalor within the back streets of the New Town and in Lothian Road, he did, however, find a certain amount of positive pleasure. Jamaica Street which runs at the immediate rear of Heriot Row is still a pretty alarming finger of squalor thrust into the interstices of the respectability of the New Town. It is still fairly vivid of a Friday and a Saturday evening. It is not difficult to imagine what it must have been like in Stevenson's day. It must have been terrific. And the back rooms of Heriot Row looked out upon it! We know that Stevenson frequented and liked the curious minuscule pubs of Jamaica Street. But it was in the avenues down to Leith, and in the clustering streets under the shadow of the Calton Hill that he found his true escape. Here was a forbidden quarter to which decent people did not go. Here, almost within hailing distance of Princes Street, was a completely defined other world. Once you entered it the bar was down between you and what you had left behind you. You were free.

Within this area, which was Stevenson's most constant and reliable escape from the world which he was evading, he was a regular, inquisitive, conspicuous, yet, at the same time, personally unobtrusive visitor. Everyone knew him by sight, everyone called him by the same nick-name of "Velvet Coat". It is to be presumed that those who were inquilines rather than visitors recognized his difference from the general crowd in which he moved in this part of Edinburgh. Yet, with a proper respect for the conventions of their milieu (and this we have on his own recorded authority) they never questioned his right to be amongst them. His affairs were his own affairs.

He was, at one and the same time, outside the crowd yet in it without being of it. They recognized his desire to be amongst them as his sole and rightful passport to their society. That he wanted to be with them and amongst them was enough for them. They did not question either his oddity of appearance or his peculiarity of manner. His patent honesty of purpose was sufficient.

He went much to public houses, of course, but he was never a deep or consistent drinker. He was too frail, and he was born a little too late to have been one of the great old school of gustful Scottish topers. Nor, on the other hand, did his temperament induce in him the easy vice of tippling or dram drinking. His imagination provided enough intoxication for his eager mind. The mere act of absorbing alcohol was not wicked to him—otherwise it might have been attractive. He had been brought up in a strictly religious home, but it was very far from being teetotal. He had been accustomed to wine since childhood; and his father kept a good cellar. It is easy to see from his works that his attitude towards drinking was childishly innocent. He makes his characters either drink nothing at all, or, as in *The Wrong Box*, drink such a fantastic amount that it is obvious that he really had little personal knowledge of the effects of drink. He obviously enjoyed "the glass that cheers" and loved good wine. But it is doubtful whether he was ever drunk in the whole of his life. His descriptions of the speech and behaviour of drunken men show keen observation and appreciation, but they somehow lack the note of experience.

He also frequented places (dives as we would now call them) where low characters and criminals used to consort. We have no need to rely on hearsay and tradition here, for he is quite explicit on this point in his writing. He is doubly explicit, or at least explicit at two different times and in two different ways. When he first wrote about himself haunting the society of thieves, vagrant seamen and those whose habitations were continually being moved by the police, he is still under the influence of his romantic attitude towards these people, even though he assumes a slightly deprecating air of disapproval —not towards his associates but towards his own folly. Then, in after years, when he is clearly recalling one of these howffs in *The Misadventures of John Nicholson* he is inclined to laugh at the whole *mise en scene*, "the maculate linen" of Collette's midnight Shebeen, the second-rate daredevilry of the clientèle and so on, rather in the manner of one who is anxious to point out that he has seen a good deal of the rest of the world since those early days. For my part, I prefer the earlier recollection, partly because it is more evocative, and partly because (though romantically written about) it is more likely to be true.

"I see now the little sanded kitchen where Velvet Coat (for that was the name I went by) has spent days together, generally in silence, and making sonnets in a penny version book; and, rough as the material may appear, I do not believe these days were amongst the least happy I have spent. I was distinctly petted. The women were most kind and gentle to me. . . ."

All this, though seen through R.L.S.'s unshakably kindly recollection, has the ring of truth about it.

"The women were most kind and gentle" to him he has said. And it is certain that he was kind and gentle to them. If the youthful R.L.S. made no very strong social or moral distinctions between his male companions upon these expeditions into the underworld of his city, he would be even less likely to be censorious about the women whom he found there. Indeed, in this matter all his romanticism would come well to the fore. The impetus that drove this mid-Victorian youth to throw off the shackles of his upbringing and seek the comfort of these places was a poetic if slightly phthisical fever which had a touch of chivalry about it. R.L.S. would have been ready to play the role of Des Grieux to any Manon Lescaut.

Stevenson's attitude towards sex has come in for a good part of the discussion that has gone on about the period of his early revolt. And, as in all the rest of it, exaggerated and contrary views have been the order of the day. Some people think that to have a dispute at all on the matter is unseemly and unnecessary. I cannot agree. The amorous (in the full sense of the word) life of a man of genius and of passion is surely of importance to those who are interested in him. And, when one is dealing with a subject such as I am here, the early and rebellious existence of R.L.S. against the background of Edinburgh, it would be preposterous, almost prurient to omit mention of the subject.

In the days of my boyhood and youth during and just after the 1914-18 war, there were prevalent amongst the more outspoken masculine circles in Edinburgh, obviously exaggerated, but highly persistent legends about R.L.S.'s sexual virility. And all sorts of unlikely stories of this kind were fathered on him by the "anti-sentimentalists" and the sentimentalists alike. Posthumous gossip of this sort is likely to spring up about any writer with so definite a moral reputation as Stevenson had imposed upon him after his death. It was more than likely to occur if the background to that reputation was late-Victorian Edinburgh. I discount ninety per cent. of such stories: I discounted them even at the time of hearing them. They were obviously partly inspired by the newly found reaction against the myth of R.L.S. the plaster saint. They were given continual new life by the peregrinations of that odd individual who toured Scotland claiming, upon the strength of a remarkable physical resemblance to be Stevenson's "by-blow" by an early Scottish love. It is now generally supposed that this individual was a fraud, deliberate or self-deceiving. He probably was, for, as I hope to show in what I have to say about Stevenson's attitude towards women, it is almost incredible that R.L.S. should have disowned a child of his. At any rate, this individual, apart from arousing a good deal of interesting speculation, has justified himself by inspiring that admirable and moving novel by Miss G. B. Stern, *No Son of Mine*.

These stories, I am quite convinced, are highly exaggerated, salacious in origin, and give a wholly erroneous impression of Stevenson's character, however near or far from the truth they may be on the score of his virility. I am equally convinced, from what one knows about the man from more reliable sources than these Edinburgh gossips, from what one feels about him, that there must have been a certain amount of fire behind this distorting column of smoke of talk. I am convinced too, that those critics, who, judging him solely by the necessarily constricted medium of his fiction, suppose him to have had low sexual powers, and that those admirers of his genius who cannot bear the thought that their hero could ever have had any sexual experience before he married his already divorced wife, are all equally wide of the mark.

At the risk of seeming to repeat myself, I may say that, at this point, I can imagine the decent Edinburgh reader who has achieved the feat of following me thus far, laying aside the book with the thought of how-beside-the-point-this-all-is! "Is this," I can imagine him or her saying, "just another of these essays in semi-fictional gossip of the kind which have recently been poured out about Burns and Edinburgh?" Let me ask any one of my fellow-citizens who may feel this, to have patience with me for a few more pages, for it is not Stevenson's youthful hot-bloodedness, nor the obscure details of his early amours that are my chief interests, my primary subjects in this chapter, but the decency of his mentality, the lovableness of character during these stressful Edinburgh days.

The details are not important, the large fact of Stevenson's mind and behaviour at this time is. At this date it is useless to speculate on the mysterious novel *Claire*, the story of a street walker, written by R.L.S. and subsequently destroyed either by his wife or by himself at the instigation of his wife. However poignantly one may regret the irreparable loss of what along with *Weir of Hermiston* may have been one of the most honest, the most truly Stevensonian products of Stevenson's pen, there is no point in debating whether, in the novel, Claire was supposed to walk the streets of Paris, London, or Edinburgh; for we shall never know now. All we can be fairly certain of is that the prototype from which she was drawn came from Edinburgh. We cannot tell now whether Stevenson's earliest and intensest love was an Edinburgh working-class girl or the blacksmith's daughter out at Swanston, or both—(possibly both; for Stevenson was capable, as I have said, not only of behaving like Manon Lescaut's des Grieux, but also of being the young, romantic, rustic lover, possibly even at the same time)—but we do know that he had the experience of love with such a girl or girls. Nor is there any point in doing as the more strenuous rearguard fighters of the R.L.S. plaster-saint myth have done in introducing the complication of a third and more respectable love in Stevenson's own social circle.

What is certain is that he enjoyed and endured an intense love for someone drawn from a class looked upon as quite impossible by his family, we do know that his behaviour and his sentiments in the throes of this love were, however passionate and physical, chivalrous, and, in intention, self-sacrificing. We know that he has drawn deeply upon his recollections of this love in *Catriona*, in *Weir of Hermiston* and in other places in his writing. For a student of his life, it is this that makes his amours at this period important: this that makes it worth while trying to reconstruct an image of his behaviour and his feeling at the time.

From his early youth until his death, Stevenson took a romantic view of the life around him. Everything was vivid, clear-cut, highly coloured and exciting. Having sought solace from the conventional world of Edinburgh, whose constriction his very excitability of temperament probably inclined him to exaggerate, he easily invested the world of his escape with a romantic glamour. The people in this new world were kind and tolerant to him, above all they were novel, they were strange. Therefore, with the eyes, not only of gratitude, but of the poet, he was quick to see in them virtues which they certainly may have had but which were not so obvious to the other more mundane Edinburgh pleasure seekers who came down on the Avernian path to drink, to "womanize" and generally to relax. In the public houses, in the flaring lights, in the ill-lit kitchens with their sanded floors and their company of semi-outlawed vagrants, amongst women of the town, he, partly defiantly, partly romantically, discovered human qualities which the rest of Edinburgh would indignantly deny.

At the same time he was no fool about this new world he had discovered. In a moment of deep depression, verging on despair, at or just after this period, he compares himself with Robert Fergusson the Edinburgh poet and calls himself "weak and vicious". This was unfair both to Fergusson and himself. For Fergusson was weak—he had little chance to be anything else—but he was not vicious. R.L.S., fundamentally, was neither. And, for all his romanticism, for all the colour of contrast that he saw in his revolt, he had an honest power of observation and a keen and active intelligence. He knew perfectly well what was the outcome of most of the public house tippling which he saw around him in the Lothian Road and in Leith Walk. Indeed he has a telling passage on it in his *Edinburgh, Picturesque Notes* which was published when he was still a young man. He knew that the camaraderie of the thieves and vagabonds whose society and whose talk fascinated him, was nothing much more than a conspiracy enforced by adversity—a conspiracy which was not based on loyalty, but could be dissolved by changing and more propitious circumstances. And above all he was, of course, well aware that a woman who sells the pleasure of her body either in the romantic role of a courtesan or by showing herself in the public street, is not a fit subject for sentimentality. But he was prepared to take romantic pleasure in the strangeness of the topsy-turvy world in which these people lived.

Sentimentality! It may seem to some that that was precisely the failing of which Stevenson was guilty in such matters. Sentimental is how they would describe the celebrated passage in his essay on the artist, the passage on the unsuccessful *"fille de joie"* pitifully hawking her unregarded charms through a heedless crowd. If they accept as true, which I do, the highly likely tradition that he loved a girl from this class in his early days in Edinburgh and wished to marry her; if, as there is much evidence to support, he recollected his love for her in the novel *Claire* and subsequently allowed the manuscript to be destroyed, they would put down both the action and the destruction to the action and reaction of sentimentality. I strongly dissent. I believe Stevenson's attitude towards women in general was chivalrous and protective and sprang not from false feeling but from a generous masculine nature. Moreover, I believe that his attitude towards that type of woman usually described as "fallen" was truly, and not unctuously, humane; it was (though he might not have relished such an epithet in his early and "free-thinking" days) Christian.

It is probable that Stevenson inherited and acquired from his much misunderstood father this chivalry towards women. Thomas Stevenson really did (though one scarcely dares to write the word nowadays for fear of mockery) venerate the sex that had given him his mother and his wife. This veneration was, as were some of his other deeper feelings, particularly his religion, touched with morbidity. So firm was his respect, so much a part of his heart was his veneration for all womankind that he could not bring himself to believe that any woman became abandoned to vice and prostitution by reasons of her own inclination, weakness or folly. His sense of guilt which, in regard to his faith was a personal matter, was here enlarged to include the whole of his own sex. He thought that all "fallen women" had fallen by the evil machinations of men alone, by man's power of seduction, by his false promises and by his subsequent oppression. He could not bring himself to believe that there were amongst women (particularly his own countrywomen) any who had become women of the streets, either professional or amateur, just because they were wanton, lazy, vicious, or merely were "lovers of the game".

Hardly any men who move much about in their own kind can be found who hold such a belief today. Modern fiction, modern drama, and the modern cinema have enlightened them if they have not improved them. But in mid-Victorian Edinburgh, the type certainly did exist, though it was uncommon. It is easy to smile nowadays at Thomas

Stevenson's naïve beliefs. But however mistaken they may have been, they did emanate from a generous and chivalrous idea. It is characteristic of the modern attitude towards the integrity of such ideas that some recent writers on the Stevenson family have, without a shred of evidence save that Thomas Stevenson was charitably interested in a "Magdalen Home", put forward the theory that his point of view in this matter came from a personal sense of guilt. They have to believe, or tell themselves that they believe, that he had ruined some innocent girl or had been dissipated in his youth. They cannot or will not accept that the charity that he gave may have been the product of a charitable impulse alone. It is a really lamentable example of how the meanness of posterity may twist and deform the most generous and genuine of men's impulses and emotions.

Thomas Stevenson may have had streaks of morbidness and even, in his dour Scottish way, of sentimentality in his character; he had, however, a very good brain. This, too, his son inherited from him, but without the morbidness and sentimentality. Moreover, even as a young man, he had seen more of the underworld than his father was ever to see in his whole life. His keen observation as well as his intellect must soon have disabused him of the notion, if ever he had it, that all of woman's misfortunes were due to man's villainy. He did, however, preserve the inherited sentiment from which his father's exaggerated ideas sprang. He did really love and respect womankind. No experience, no careful reasoning could expunge so radical a part of his mind and his emotions.

I presume that anyone who is sufficiently interested to read this book must be fairly conversant with the better known of Stevenson's novels. It is only to the novels, therefore, that I make an appeal for evidence in support of this contention. I pass over (with two exceptions which I shall quote later on) the less known letters and the even lesser known poems discovered in the 1920s. I refer the reader only to the memory of Catriona, of Flora in *St. Ives*, of the women in *Weir of Hermiston*, and even the short glimpse of the lass at Queensferry in *Kidnapped*, a book written in the first place for young boys. If he does not agree that these are portraits of women drawn by a real lover of the sex whose love was inspired by an ineradicably romantic (not sentimental) attitude towards women, there is no way in which I can make my point clearer.

These portraits occur in works which Stevenson intended to give to the world as the product of his imagination only. He was not concerned with giving himself away, however much he may have done so without meaning to. In his letters (even in the emasculated versions which the public has been allowed to read), and in his poems, in particular the semi-suppressed ones which only came to the public some thirty years after his death, he is more explicit. These letters and these poems have been combed and analysed with some zeal and industry by the anti-plaster-sanctifiers. It is not for me to regurgitate and chew once again the cud of their satisfaction. I may, perhaps, be allowed to quote twice in support of my theme about Stevenson's attitude towards women. The first is from a letter to a young art student:—

> "Whatever you do, see that you don't sacrifice a woman; that is where all imperfect loves conduct us. At the same time (if you can make it convenient to be chaste) for God's sake avoid the primness of your virtue. Hardness to a poor harlot is a sin lower than the ugliest unchastity."

This is surely a condensed version of the Stevenson (father and son) view of women. "That is where all imperfect loves conduct us" is all Thomas Stevenson. "If you can make it *convenient* to be chaste . . ." and what follows is pure R.L.S.

The second quotation comes from one of his more recently discovered poems. It is the first stanza of a poem to an unborn child, called "God gave to me a child in part":—

> "God gave to me a child in part,
> Yet wholly gave the father's heart:
> Child of my soul, O whither now
> Unborn, unmothered, goest thou?"

It is impossible to say when these touching lines, so poignantly and paradoxically characteristic of the author of *A Child's Garden of Verses*, were written. One can, however, without going into unnecessarily laborious and untasteful details, assert with near certainty that they refer to an episode in Stevenson's life well before his marriage to Fanny Osbourne. If, as is generally supposed by the more level-headed critics, they are concerned with something that happened to Stevenson during his early and wandering life in Edinburgh, no comment is needed here.

Indeed, I do not feel inclined to make any further remarks about either of these two quotations from Stevenson's private and semi-private writings. If they do not speak for themselves nothing that I can say about them will make them any more explicit.

Stevenson's romantic view of the pleasures of low life estranged him from more than strictly the respectable circles of Edinburgh. Their distate for his course of life at this time was natural and to be understood. He must have expected it and possibly even enjoyed certain aspects of it. What did really make him feel lonely, however, was that (with the possible exception of his cousin Bob Stevenson) he could find no kindred spirits amongst any fellow-Avernians in his Heine-like attitude to life and ladies of the streets. Incidentally, it is worth remembering that the wife of Professor Fleeming Jenkins, the first woman of his own class to understand him, called him "The young Heine with a Scottish accent". Edinburgh young men of the comfortable classes who, on Saturday nights or after football matches, seek the relaxations of Leith Walk and the like, have always taken a strictly realistic attitude towards the pleasures of the bottle and the bed. They suffer little remorse and seem to enjoy no romance. It is so to-day. It was so two hundred years ago in the days of James Boswell. It was so when R.L.S. was a young man. Boswell was troubled by a conscience: Stevenson was haunted by romance. Both were lonely.

Stevenson's loneliness at this period of his life has been, if one may use such a figure of speech, protracted into posterity. It seems to me that very few of the many who have written about him after his death have been capable of understanding or have even taken the trouble to try and understand what he was seeking in these early Edinburgh days. Amidst the welter of misunderstanding about the young Stevenson which I have dwelt on earlier in this book, nothing is so ludicrously wide of the mark as the attempt that some have made to sentimentalize him in his rebellion.

One laborious but fairly well known life of Stevenson which gained a good deal of notice in the 1920's contains some ridiculous examples of this. The author of this life has honestly attempted an objective view of his subject but displays an abysmal ignorance of, or lack of feeling for, Edinburgh types and what they must have meant to R.L.S. in his young days. He discovers in a series of stock generalizations the usual misapprehensions about the Edinburgh upper classes and their "unbending puritanism" and so on. But it is when he comes to humbler Edinburgh folk that he takes a real toss. He makes out a case for Stevenson being in love with an Edinburgh prostitute of Highland origin whom he attempted to reform, and who was in love with him. He puts down R.L.S.'s early affection for the Highlands and the Gaelic way of life to the probability that while he lay in this Celtic charmer's arms she told him old Highland tales and together they sang the songs of the north, which may have implanted in him the idea of writing *Over the Sea to Skye*! If such an effort at community singing ever did take place between Stevenson and one of his hypothetical doxies the theme of the song was much more likely to have been *The Ball of Kirriemuir* than anything approaching *Over the Sea to Skye*.

There is also printed, extant, and to be read in libraries, a novel by the same author, the subject of which is the same hypothetical, but (it must be admitted) possible love affair between R.L.S. and the Highland girl. The imagination neither boggles nor reels at the thought of what Stevenson would say if he could read it. It retreats into discreet obscurity and profound silence.

Yes, poor Stevenson's posthumous reputation has been the subject of almost unlimited sentimentality, sentimentality that takes as its themes his earliest days in Edinburgh and his last in the South Seas. It is with some slight hesitation, therefore, that I have ventured to interpret his romanticism at the period of his life under discussion. I hesitate even more before concluding by trying to express what I think he felt about his early and, to put it mildly, unconventional love affairs at this time. I cannot resist doing so, however, for two reasons. The first is that, recollecting my own youth in Edinburgh—that grey, yet highly coloured, that austere, yet abundantly romantic city, so harsh and yet so beneficent a background to the pains and pleasures of the greensickness of first love—I feel a sympathy for R.L.S. that somehow makes me believe that I know what he felt. The second is that I cannot recall that any who have written about Stevenson at this time have done so save from the objective point of view. They have lacked the inclination or the hardihood or the knowledge to attempt a truly sympathetic approach—or perhaps it is just that they have been too wise to try such a thing.

The pursuit and the salvation of love amongst frail women is, of course, a favourite theme of romantic poetry and fiction. But it *is* poetry and it *is* fiction. In fact and in life very few men of the comfortable classes who seek relaxation amongst these frail women ever think of finding love in such circumstances. Why then, did Stevenson so ardently pursue love in the shadows of his town and time? Was it purely a matter of his rebellious and paradoxical temperament? Would he have behaved as he did behave in any other city in Europe at any time in the nineteenth century? I wonder. I think not. And, since the subject of this book is R L.S.

and Edinburgh—Edinburgh alone, I allow my wonderment to express itself in print.

The ordinary drab of the Edinburgh street is, and I imagine, has been for a long time, a pitiful creature. She, even more than her sister in London, and ever so much more than her cousin in Paris, is a creature of the twilight. She seeks the twilight not only because it is merciful but because it is suitable to her. You feel that it has made her, and that it is her proper background—a background thoughtfully provided by the poor civic lighting of the town. How, then, could the young, ardent and amorous as well as sensuously romantic young Stevenson have fallen in love with such a one? He might have loved her in the true, the Christian, the charitable sense of the word. He might in the obscurity of a Rose Street pub, and with all the decorations of a romantic gesture (which would not have deprived the gesture of its validity) have proclaimed "he that is without sin among you, let him first cast a stone at her". And how well he might have enjoyed saying it. But could he have fallen in love with her? Could she have haunted his mind, his imagination and his recollection as did the (let us be honest) hypothetical Claire?

Of course he could not. But then there is, has been, and will be for a long time, another type of East of Scotland and Edinburgh girl who lives upon the borderland of respectability and disrepute. For a man of sensuous rather than sensual imagination, she is immensely alluring. She has in her countenance, in her bearing and in her manner an intoxicating mixture of primness and abandon, rectitude and ribaldry, of shyness and shameless laughter.

It is in her mouth that this combination of unexpected but not clashing qualities is most clearly discovered. She has a complexion that would be the envy of the women of the world, if they could see it, and a figure of straightforward, if somewhat stolid appeal. But it is in her mouth that all her essence lies. The upper lip is straight, almost compressed. The lower lip is full and tremulous with readiness for laughter and for licence. And it is the mouth of a loyal person. I have not seen its like anywhere else. Were I a painter in the part of the world where I live, I should devote a disproportionately large amount of my time and talents to portraying such faces with such mouths—but I am not a painter. I can only write down what I feel about them.

I feel, and what I feel is worth no more than my feeling, that it was someone of this kind whom Stevenson loved in Edinburgh and *of* Edinburgh eighty years ago. What witness can I call to support my feeling? Only one. Catriona.

CHAPTER VII

For at least two hundred and fifty years Edinburgh has been continuously full of vivid, highly individual, yet characteristic Edinburgh types. This does not mean only the eccentrics already mentioned. The lawyers, the old ladies, the shopgirls, the working men, the ministers, the waiters and waitresses, the domestic servants, the Judges of the Court of Session would have been, and would still be very taken aback if they had heard or were to hear themselves called eccentrics. They were and are just Edinburgh folk.

It is strange how much Edinburgh novelists, or people who have written fiction about Edinburgh, have neglected the richness of this raw material for their art or craft—a raw material quite as ample as that to be found in Glasgow or the Highlands, in which parts fiction writers have tumbled over themselves in an excess of zeal to portray local character. There have been no visiting fiction writers who have attempted the Edinburgh character; and, with some exceptions, such as Dr. John Brown in his book *Rab and his Friends*, few natives who have succeeded. Most novelists and story-tellers about Edinburgh are content (however convincing their major character, however well contrived their plots) to fill in their backgrounds with descriptions of the romantic physical scene and with a set of unconvincing stock "Scotch characters". This is odd, for Edinburgh conversation is full of stories about the "Edinburgh type" in all classes; and Edinburgh painters since the days of Allan Ramsay have continuously delighted in portraying the unmistakable Scottish and Edinburgh face. They, at least, were well aware of their good fortune in having at their disposal such a wealth of natural models. Only two novelists have rivalled the painters in this respect—Scott and Stevenson.

Of these two Stevenson is the more satisfying. This is not because his powers of observation and portrayal were more powerful. It is merely that Edinburgh filled a larger place in his mind than it did in Scott's. Scott's immense imagination roamed all over Europe, and, even in the Scottish novels, all over Scotland. The magnificent first half of *The Heart of Midlothian* is certainly Edinburgh, and an Edinburgh drawn from Scott's own observations and reminiscences; so are certain scenes in *Guy Mannering*. The characters are unmistakable Lowland and East of Scotland types without question, but they are Scottish first, and only Edinburgh incidentally. None of them, it must be admitted, is as unmistakably of Edinburgh as is the immortal Baillie Nicol Jarvie of Glasgow and of Glasgow alone.

Stevenson, on the other hand, lingered over Edinburgh in his writings with an obvious gusto for the city and its people. He brought Edinburgh into all his Scottish novels, even when there appeared to be no necessity from the point of view of the plot to do so. The scene of *The Master of Ballantrae*, for instance, is set entirely between the west coast of Scotland and North America; yet a large part of the force of the drama of this great story comes from the fact that it is seen through the eyes and told in the words of that obvious son of Edinburgh, Mr. Ephraim MacKellar. Some critics have found it impossible to believe that so prosaic a creature as they conceive MacKellar to have been could have told the story in so gripping a manner. No one, who from experience of Edinburgh knows the true MacKellar type, would agree. The conflict in MacKellar's character of a dry-as-dust background and training with a romantic capacity for devotion leading him almost into gullibility is pure Edinburgh, and corresponds to the purely Glasgow conflict of business instincts and Highland pride which makes Walter Scott's Baillie Nicol Jarvie ring so truly down the centuries from the time at which Rob Roy was supposed to be set. Stevenson was not only being dramatically effective in choosing MacKellar as his mouthpiece, he was true to type, and all the more true because he loved writing about it.

This pleasure in portraying Edinburgh people of all kinds is so obvious in his pictures of the more celebrated characters of the Scottish and Edinburgh novels that it conveys itself to the reader infectiously even if he is ignorant of the city. Despite their differences, they are all products of the same town or environment. They are not only wonderfully alive and memorable, they are as recognizable as Raeburn's portraits. David Balfour in *Kidnapped*, for all his rusticity, is an Edinburgh lad up from the country. His lawyer, Rankeillor, is the first of a long list of Edinburgh legal types on which R.L.S. delighted to linger. He was followed by the villainous Simon Fraser (a shrewd and well-noted Highland introduction into the Edinburgh scene), by the tremendous Grant of Prestongrange and many others, culminating in the greatest of them all, Lord Hermiston.

Now the point about these many legal personalities scattered throughout Stevenson's works, is this. They are all, whether they dominate the story, or only slip into it, distinct, different from each other and unforgettable; yet all and each of them are of the city and of nowhere else. It is the same with the women. Miss Gilchrist in *St. Ives*, her niece Flora, the landlady in the same book, Miss Grant of Prestongrange in *Catriona*, Mrs. Weir of Hermiston and a dozen others, gentle or simple, severe or alluring, dragon-like or douce, they are all individuals, all of them characters, yet all of them of Edinburgh. This is not only excellent story-telling and excellent art, it is thoroughly refreshing for any Edinburgh reader who has grown accustomed to the dreary spectacle of his vivid, vital townsfolk marching like stock puppets through the usual Edinburgh story or play.

How tired one gets of reading in fiction or seeing upon the stage Edinburgh characters who seem to be made all according to a set of patterns. The dragon-like old ladies are dragon-like from their severe countenances right down into the core of their hearts. The douce young ladies are nauseatingly sweet all through—pure saccharine. The dry-as-dust lawyers are composed of nothing but dust. The humorous individuals never speak save through the medium of pawky humour. The brutes are always brutal, and stern parents are never anything but stern.

There is nothing of this in Stevenson. What makes his Edinburgh people so alive, so convincing, is the fact that their creator is not content with merely observing and describing in a wonderfully accurate way their appearances, their mannerisms of behaviour and speech: he does something more. He goes deep into their characters; he searches out the cherished and carefully hidden places of their minds and their affections. He revels in the complexities and high contrasts of the Scottish and Edinburgh personality—qualities which are a continual delight to the observer of the human scene in this city, qualities which are (in Stevenson's books) surely a delight to any reader of fiction in English, whether he knows Edinburgh or not.

David Balfour, in *Kidnapped*, comes before us at first as a gawky, uncouth, reserved Lowland lad newly come to town, full of native caution reinforced by Whiggish tuition, the kind of figure usually accepted as the typical unemotional plodding "lad o' pairts". Soon he begins to show a capacity for romantic loyalty and discovers in himself a world of emotional possibilities which we would never have suspected at the start of the tale. In the culmination of his story in *Catriona*, he is in love so convincingly and so poignantly that he seems to speak for the love-sick youth that lies hidden somewhere in all men. And yet (here is the truth as well as the art in the portrayal of this character) all this development of emotion is subtly and almost imperceptibly revealed. It is revealed so gently that it does not destroy our original conception of him. In the end, after we have endured, and hoped, and longed, and suffered and loved in sympathy with him, he remains in essence as he began—a decent Lowland Edinburgh Whig, without airs or graces. If you found him a trifle sententious, ponderous and irritating when you first made his acquaintance, you still do when you take leave of him—and this despite the fact that it is from his mouth, through his eyes, and in his experiences and emotions we have heard one of the great romances written in the nineteenth century.

How evocative of certain sides of the Scottish and Edinburgh character this all is. And how acutely R.L.S. must have observed it in his boyhood and youth in order to be able to transmit and describe it with such faithful art later on. MacKellar, the narrator of *The Master of Ballantrae*, to whom I have already referred, is another example of this effective use of the complexity of the Lowland Scottish character. I am not sure that MacKellar is not a more skilful piece of work than David Balfour. One's sympathies are less easily stirred by a middle-aged pedant (however human we may discover him to be) than by a gawky, oafish country lad who at least has the appeal of wide-eyed youth upon his side. David lingers in one's memory more easily than does MacKellar partly by reason of this appeal, and partly because he is the central figure of the narrative in which he appears; and MacKellar is not. But to conceive of MacKellar, to put him on paper, to make him sympathetic, is possibly a bolder task than to do the same for David. It certainly is the work of a more mature writer. The dichotomy in David's character is very effectively drawn. But the dichotomy in MacKellar is more subtle. The combination of an awkward manner and a romantic and loving heart is more difficult to achieve in an imaginary middle-aged "dry-as-dust" than in a hobbledehoy. But how vivid and true to town and type both characters are.

Stevenson discovers the same skill in the same technique when introducing us to all his other Edinburgh characters, whether major or minor, important or unimportant. Always there is the contrasting and unsuspected undercurrent in them, the other side so carefully concealed beneath the superficially obvious type. The great Prestongrange, in *Catriona*, beneath his apparently ruthless political opportunism, hides a conscience and a kind heart. His daughter, Barbara Grant, shows to the world the accepted character of an upper-class, eighteenth-century Edinburgh miss, full of polite mockery, but there soon emerges in her a heart as tender and as sentimental as that of a nineteenth-century romantic. The landladies, the respectable old women, the inferior lawyers, even the rascals, all are shown to lead a double and hidden life of which the undertones are virtue or vice, tenderness or rectitude.

Even the greatest creation of them all, Lord Hermiston, seems to us at the beginning to be no more than a bully of distinction, a brute in a high place. In the end, or near the broken end of this unfinished masterpiece, we feel (however unsympathetic we may be to him) that we are as much in the presence of an antique Roman as of a Scot. We even feel that this intimidating, coarse anachronism from a more brutal age, this man who scorns suffering in others, has deeply suffered and still suffers in himself. His own silence on the matter, and the restraint of his creator in no more than hinting at it only serve to make our knowledge of it all the more impressive.

Weir of Hermiston is a character so overpowering as to be repellent to some readers. It is difficult to think that the gentle and hypersensitive Stevenson created him out of his own imagination. The answer is, of course, that he did nothing of the kind. With all the skill and the art of a modern Phidias, but dealing in greyer, more sombre material than that at the disposal of the Greek, he hewed him out of the unchanging rock and stone of Edinburgh.

Hermiston is the greatest character in all Stevenson, greater than Long John Silver, greater than the Master of Ballantrae, greater than many others better known than Hermiston, greater even than Alan Breck Stewart. Only Kirsty Elliot threatens his pre-eminence: and she comes out of the same book as Hermiston. It was the last book that Stevenson wrote. He wrote it separated by half the surface of the world and at a long distance in time from his native Scotland and Edinburgh. Over fifteen years had passed since he could be said to have really lived in Edinburgh. Many experiences, many strange countries, hundreds of new acquaintances had been crowded into those fifteen years. Even his keen, acquisitive, inquisitive nature must have been nearly flooded with the ever changing novelty. Yet, for his greatest and last work he turned for inspiration (and never did his inspiration answer him with greater clarity and strength) to the city of his birth and of his youth. This is not only a sign of his astonishing power of retentive and detailed observation over a period of years, it is a tribute to the power of that city over his mind and heart.

There is little or no evidence to show that, when Stevenson was actually living in Edinburgh, he paid much attention to the characters of the town that emerge with such striking fidelity in his later works. Even his celebrated long essay, *Edinburgh, Picturesque Notes*, was written after he had begun to stray away from his native city. Moreover, though it builds up a highly evocative picture of Edinburgh, it does so mainly by means of atmosphere and by a description of what the place looks like and feels like. There is little reference in it to persons and personalities—little that is to say, for one who was afterwards to create David Balfour, Prestongrange, Barbara Grant, Mrs. Weir and Adam Weir of Hermiston.

The truth is that, from his adolescence, almost up to the time of leaving Edinburgh, Stevenson felt none of that ardent curiosity for his city of the kind that Dickens, for instance, felt as a boy and a youth for London. He was lonely, and felt that loneliness keenly. He was, if far from being an outcast from his own social circle, an obvious peculiarity, and would have been peculiar and odd in any conventional society of his town and time. He may, out of bravado, have exaggerated this tendency to peculiarity, but he resented the fact that it should have been forced upon him.

He was always doing odd, even if quite innocent things to try and escape from the ordinary Edinburgh surroundings. He and his cousin Bob Stevenson carried on a world of make-believe imaginary characters such as the fictitious German Herr Libbel. This creature of the two cousins' imagination was supposed to have pawned goods all over Edinburgh; and they would harry various pawnshops and other tradesmen's establishments with inquiries about Mr. Libbel, so as to try and persuade people that this creature of their joking dream world really existed. When people found out about it they thought it all rather silly, and, in their heavy-mannered way, said so. All this kind of thing is a clear indication that, in his youth, R.L.S. found Edinburgh irksome. If he could not escape from it in fact, he could escape from it by being different from everybody else and by the inventions of his own imagination.

But we do not need such fragmentary pieces of evidence to tell us of his feelings towards Edinburgh at this time. There are plenty of people who have remembered and recorded what he said about it in his youth. Miss Rosaline Masson, for instance, his most conscientious and well-informed biographer, herself a citizen of the town, says that he used to abuse and revile the city and its inhabitants. He was averse to the society of his fellow-students who were contemptuous of him. He had little use for any of his schoolfellows from "the Academy" who remembered him, and, amongst his own society or that of his parents, consorted only with those older than himself, those who, like the Fleeming Jenkins, showed enough imagination and sympathy to understand what lay at the back of his oddities. He had, it is true, Bob Stevenson and Henley and Baxter as ardent companions of his own age at this time. But Bob was a fellow-rebel. Henley was an oddity as well as being an Englishman and a stranger. And Baxter, well Baxter, the good faithful Baxter, was just Baxter, something of a foil, one suspects, to the other three.

To rebel against the town of their youth, to revile it when young, is not an uncommon habit of men of genius, imagination, or even of talent. Many men of far less imagination and talent than R.L.S. had, have rebelled against Edinburgh and said all manner of harsh things about her when they were young. She has been richly abused by her own sons as well as by those who have been sent from the south to be exiled in her. Edinburgh is a very definite city. It is difficult to be indifferent to her. You either love her, or are annoyed and angry with her to the point of active dislike. She is, on the whole, unsympathetic to urgent imaginative young people who not only want their own way but who want to make a splash while getting it. She is unsympathetic too, in a particularly irritating way. For she just glacially ignores them. She is too much of a capital to show that she is shocked by them. She is too respectable (or, to put it more charitably) too formally well mannered to pay any attention to them.

And yet, and yet the force of her character is so strong that she makes an indelible impression on the minds of all such young people who have rebelled against her and who have reviled her when they lived in her. In after years these rebels find that it is impossible to shake the memory of her from them, difficult even to escape from the mould into which she has cast the shape of their youthful years. In later life they return to her either in imagination, in conversation, or in fact. They find they can recall, as if it were yesterday, that now distant irritation, anger and sense of frustration that she once provoked in them. But now all these past emotions are swallowed up in admiration or perhaps even in some tenderness of feeling. For all her one-time harshness, she has made them what they were when they were young. She is as much a part of them as they are of her, and there is no escaping the fact, even if they wished to do so. They bow their middle-aged heads in respect before her grand immutability and feel, quite personally, a little proud of her. Should they now hear anyone abusing her or reviling her, they will just smile. They will not bother to defend her, for they know that she has no need of their defence and would pay as little attention to it as once she did to their own remote rebellion.

R.L.S., who had to pack so much into his comparatively short life, was quick in his emotions, quick in his reactions. It is characteristic of him that he talked of himself as middle-aged when he was in his thirties. It was perhaps natural, then, for him to go through this usual reversal of feeling towards his native city when he was, by many standards, a young man. It may be that this youthfulness in him enabled him to recall with greater clarity than do most returning wanderers (either in the flesh or in the imagination) the sharp scenes and sounds, and, above all, the people of Edinburgh. But this cannot have been the only reason. For the further he got from Edinburgh in time and place, the more accurately does he seem to be able to evoke the city of his memories. It is not only his nostalgia that was becoming the more acute, it was his power for seeing and hearing the place again. The further he travelled from it, the more closely did his youth rise up before him, visible, palpable, audible to his inner sense. And, with increasing mastery over his art, he was able to express this acuteness of his sensibility as no other writer on Edinburgh has ever done.

This vivid revocation of Edinburgh and its people in later life shows that, despite his almost self-imposed loneliness during his youth, he must, even with the eye and ear of distrust and dislike, have been noting and observing all the time. When he was first beginning to conceive of romances his imagination took him to far-off places and to distant times remote from his prosaic contemporary surroundings. But the artist in him, as well as the inquisitive observer that we know he was, must have been working, storing up impressions of character and voice that were to bear such rich fruit later on. For it is in character and voice that his creations are so markedly authentic.

The past of his city, however, had always held his imagination, had fascinated him, even when he was rebelling against its present. The past of Edinburgh was possibly just one more escape as was the underworld of the town from the Edinburgh that he conceived as surrounding and oppressing him during that rebellion. It may have been a romantic escape, but it was far from being false or tinsel. Stevenson's sense of the past was, for a confessedly romantic novelist, extraordinarily accurate and vivid. The eighteenth century that he brings to life in *Kidnapped, Catriona* and *The Master of Ballantrae* is the real eighteenth century of Edinburgh or of rural Scotland. It sounds of it: it smells of it. It was not the second-hand product of contemporary sentimental fiction. It came from authoritative as well as imaginative reading, and, perhaps, above all, from observation. R.L.S. really knew the Old Town of Edinburgh, not as an occasional tourist from the comfortable quarters, but as a frequent and lonely wanderer in it. His well known and often expressed sense of kinship with Robert Fergusson, the boy poet of the eighteenth-century Edinburgh streets (born exactly a hundred years before Stevenson), was more than a whimsical fancy. He really felt with Fergusson not only because he was, in so many ways, like him, but because he knew, by a true sense of evocation, what Fergusson's "black old town" had been like.

He also knew the countryside around Edinburgh very well. He used it too as an escape from the town society which was then uncongenial to him. The celebrated Swanston cottage which his father had taken when R.L.S. was in his teens was no prosperous city man's week-end retreat. It was, for the Stevenson family, and for R.L.S. in particular, a real country house, with its back turned on the town and its face towards the unchanging hills. In the 'sixties and 'seventies the aspect of, and many of the characters in rural Scotland (and rural Scotland began at the very gates of Edinburgh) had not suffered one-tenth of the changes that we know to-day. Stevenson loved this countryside, but again, with no false sentiment, for he really knew as well as relished its aspect and the people who lived in it. His shepherds are real Scots shepherds, of the kind who had been in the Border country for two hundred years, and were not idealized portraits. His "House of Shaws" in *Kidnapped* is no "Castle of Otranto", but a real brokendown laird's house of nameless date. He must have seen the bones of many such an establishment still standing and still rotting in his solitary wanderings near Edinburgh.

All his stories about Edinburgh, with the exception of the not very convincing *Misadventures of John Nicholson* are placed in the past—though in the last two, *St. Ives* and *Weir of Hermiston*, he approaches nearer to his own time, bringing them into the early part of the century of his own birth. Now the pre-eminent quality of these stories and novels (apart from the authentic ring of the past that they possess) is the fact that each and every character in them lives, and lives in the memory long after one has read the book. No writer, of however strong an imagination, could have spun such creatures out of his brain without the assistance of real models. They are portraits, composed portraits maybe, but skilfully composed, of real people whom R.L.S. saw and heard about him in the streets, the drawing-rooms and the law courts of the Edinburgh of his day.

It is impossible, while on the subject of Stevenson's Edinburgh characters, to refrain from yet one more mention of the Lord Justice Clerk, Weir of Hermiston, for he is the very climax of Stevenson's creations in this vein. Hermiston was admittedly based on Lord Braxfield, the famous Hanging Judge in Edinburgh at the end of the eighteenth and the beginning of the nineteenth century. Apart from a striking description of his manner and mannerisms in Lord Cockburn's *Memorials*, some grimly humorous anecdotes passed on by tradition, and the report of his speeches, we really do not know much about the character of Braxfield. He exists even to this day in Scotland as a kind of legend rather than as the memory of a real person, a legend typifying an old (but not so very distant) past, when prisoners at the High Court of Edinburgh could be jeered on their way from the dock to the hanging by odious judicial sallies from the bench, when a juryman could be exorted by the Learned Judge to "come awa, Mr. Horner and help us tae hang another o' thae damned scoondrels". We know also that he was considered a sound lawyer and was a memorable topor. But of his inner character, of what he was like at home or amongst his family and his nearest, we know nothing.

Using this traditional figure, compounded out of anecdotes and printed speeches, as a starting point for his imagination, Stevenson created his Hermiston. But Braxfield and the circumstances of his time are nothing more than a starting point. Braxfield steps off the stage and Hermiston takes complete possession, as soon as Stevenson shows us the private life of his Lord Justice Clerk, as soon as we see him at table with his shivering wife or silent son. And, by the time we see, rather than hear him suffering shame and indignity because of the supposed misdemeanour of that son, all memory of Braxfield is wiped from our minds. The model has disappeared; the portrait remains.

This is not to say that there was not another, or two or three other composite and anonymous models from whom Stevenson was drawing at memory, over a long period of time, and at the end of his life. Indeed, some ill-natured and extremely ill-informed people have gone to the length of suggesting that the picture of the Hermiston family circle is a picture of Stevenson's own home with his father in the *rôle* of Hermiston. This is, of course, nonsense, and is scarcely worth refuting. Stevenson may have taken the pattern (not an uncommon one) of his own family as the pattern for his story. Archie Weir is admittedly a somewhat idealized self-portrait, but there the Stevenson connection with the Hermiston family ends. No. Lord Hermiston was not Thomas Stevenson, nor Lord Braxfield, nor any particular judge that we know of; but that he was some one or two or three old Edinburgh legal characters lingering in Stevenson's homesick mind in his last days in the South Seas cannot be doubted.

The dialogue in the book, particularly the speech of Hermiston alone would prove it. Stevenson had an incomparably quick ear for the authentic sound of Scots speech. He could improvise on it and make it tender or brutal or forceful as he pleased. But even he could not have thought of the following description of the courtship of Adam Weir (as he then was) unless he had had some original in mind:

"But chance cast her in the path of Adam Weir, then the new Lord-Advocate, a recognized, risen man, the conqueror of many obstacles, and thus late in the day beginning to think upon a wife. He was one who looked rather to obedience than beauty, yet it would seem he was struck with her at the first look. 'Wha's she?' he said, turning to his host; and, when he had been told, 'Ay,' says he, 'she looks menseful. She minds me—'; and then, after a pause (which some have been daring enough to set down to sentimental recollections), 'Is she releegious?' he asked, and was shortly after, at his own request, presented. The acquaintance, which it seems profane to call a courtship, was pursued with Mr. Weir's accustomed industry, and was long a legend, or rather a source of legends, in the Parliament House. He was described coming, rosy with much port, into the drawing-room, walking direct up to the lady, and assailing her with pleasantries, to which the embarrassed fair one responded, in what seemed a kind of agony, 'Eh, Mr. Weir!' or 'O, Mr. Weir!' or 'Keep me, Mr. Weir!' On the very eve of their engagement, it was related that one had drawn near to the tender couple, and had overheard the lady cry out, with the tones of one who talked for the sake of talking, 'Keep me, Mr. Weir, and what became of him?' and the profound accents of the suitor reply, 'Haangit, mem, haangit.' "

Or this, the famous scene between father and son after Archie Weir has denounced capital punishment, this surely is something more than a feat of imagination. I do not suggest that Stevenson ever took part in such a scene or even witnessed it. But the words are from the mouths of real men:

" 'You're a young gentleman that doesna approve of Caapital Punishment,' said Hermiston. 'Weel, I'm an auld man that does. I was glad to get Jopp haangit, and what for would I pretend I wasna? You're all for honesty, it seems; you couldn't even steik your mouth on the public street. What for should I steik mines upon the bench, the King's officer, bearing the sword, a dreid to evil-doers, as I was from the beginning, and as I will be to the end! Mair than enough of it! Heedious! I never gave twa thoughts to heediousness, I have no call to be bonny. I'm a man that gets through with my day's business, and let that suffice.'

The ring of sarcasm had died out of his voice as he went on; the plain words became invested with some of the dignity of the Justice-seat.

'It would be telling you if you could say as much,' the speaker resumed. 'But ye cannot. Ye've been reading some of my cases, ye say. But it was not for the law in them, it was to spy out your faither's nakedness, a fine employment in a son. You're splairging; you're running at lairge in life like a wild nowt. It's impossible you should think any longer of coming to the Bar. You're not fit for it; no splairger is. And another thing: son of mines or no son of mines, you have flung fylement in public on one of the Senators of the Coallege of Justice, and I would make it my business to see that ye were never admitted there yourself. There is a kind of a decency to be observit. Then comes the next of it—what am I to do with ye next? Ye'll have to find some kind of a trade, for I'll never support ye in idleset. What do ye fancy ye'll be fit for? The pulpit? Na, they could never get diveenity into that bloackhead. Him that the law of man whammles is no likely to do muckle better by the law of God. What would ye make of hell? Wouldna your gorge rise at that? Na, there's no room for splairgers under the fower quarters of John Calvin. What else is there? Speak up. Have ye got nothing of your own?'

'Father, let me go to the Peninsula,' said Archie. 'That's all I'm fit for—to fight.'

'All? quo' he!' returned the Judge. 'And it would be enough too, if I thought it. But I'll never trust ye so near the French, you that's so Frenchifeed.'

'You do me injustice there, sir,' said Archie. 'I am loyal; I will not boast; but any interest I may have ever felt in the French—'

'Have ye been so loyal to me?' interrupted his father.

There came no reply.

'I think not,' continued Hermiston. 'And I would send no man to be a servant to the King, God bless him! that has proved such a shauchling son to his own faither. You can splairge here on the Edinburgh streets, and where's the hairm? It doesna play buff on me! And if there were twenty thousand eediots like yourself, sorrow a Duncan Jopp would hang the fewer. But there's no splairging possible in a camp; and if you were to go to it, you would find out for yourself whether Lord Well'n'ton approves of caapital punishment or not. You a sodger!' he cried, with a sudden burst of scorn. 'Ye auld wife, the sodjers would bray at ye like cuddies!'

As at the drawing of a curtain. Archie was aware of some illogicality in his position, and stood abashed. He had a strong impression, besides, of the essential valour of the old gentleman before him, how conveyed it would be hard to say.

'Well, have ye no other proposeetion?' said my lord again.

'You have taken this so calmly, sir, that I cannot but stand ashamed,' began Archie.

'I'm nearer voamiting, though, than you would fancy,' said my lord."

It would be impossible to quote a better piece of Scottish character-drawing, nor a more authentic reproduction of the Edinburgh speech in the old style than that. For anyone who knows it, it brings the old northern capital to mind with greater clarity and more force than do the pages and pages of descriptive writing that have been poured out about Edinburgh during the last hundred years.

It was written and dictated by R. L. Stevenson during the last month of his life in Samoa.

CHAPTER VIII

IN outward things Edinburgh is a city of extremes. Her castle-crowned rock and Old Town present a skyline as shamelessly theatrical and romantic as any in Europe. Her New Town is built out of austere grey stone in the austerest and yet most beautiful eighteenth-century classical style. At times she looks like a severe maiden aunt; at other times she appears to be as over-dressed as a courtesan. Though she is the capital of a small but important country, the sea and the countryside crowd up to her very gates: the transition is abrupt. That countryside is sometimes sour to look at, sometimes luxuriant. The squalor of some of her streets is alarming. The prosperity and overwhelming "style" of other of her houses and squares can, if one is in another mood, be almost equally alarming. Her climate can be painfully harsh. At the same time I do not know anything in the way of weather more beneficent than her autumn days that sometimes succeed each other in an apparently indefinite prolongation of summer. And then, with a clap and a howl the winter comes.

In this matter of extremes Edinburgh is much the same to-day as it was during Stevenson's childhood and youth. Here and there the outer town has slopped over into the country in unpleasant bungaloid growths, but not much. The march of the Edinburgh suburbs has been, on the whole, a dignified one. Here and there the squalor of the old parts has been cleaned up, but not much. The façade of squalor as well as the façade of monumental prosperity remains. So does the contrast of classicism and romanticism, of bareness and luxuriance, of howling, rain-soaked winds and long, still, sunny days, composed of that curious pale northern gold.

It is difficult not to think that these extravagant circumstances have had their effect on the people of Edinburgh. Their temperament, usually supposed by foreigners to be dour and restrained, is, in reality, given to far more extremes in depth than is that of their easier-going English neighbours. One thing is certain, and that is that the appearance, style and weather of Edinburgh helped to mould the temperament of one inhabitant of the town—young Stevenson.

Any happy, imaginative child is capable of finding the surroundings in which he lives, plays and grows up, exciting and romantic. The dreariest suburb of a gross industrial town can become a fairyland for such a one. It does not remain so, however. Adolescence and youth quickly bring disenchantment. This was not so with Stevenson. We have evidence in his writing, in the memoirs of those who knew him as a child, that soon after he reached Heriot Row, when he was only five, his imagination was genuinely seized and fired by aspects of Edinburgh which were to remain in his mind and memory all his life.

Many people born in Edinburgh have noticed one odd quality of the city. It is one of the few places where, as one grows up, childish impressions do not dwindle or decrease. We are all familiar with the experience of returning to a schoolroom where we sat as children and finding it, in after years, astonishingly, even pitifully small. We go back to Highland country where we spent our school holidays decades ago and are disappointed to find that the mountains have turned into hills. The theatre in which we were taken to see our first pantomime was not only a palace of glorious colour, it was the size of the Albert Hall. Now it is fustian and small.

This does not happen to Edinburgh. Why, I do not know, but it seems (and how often I have heard this from other contemporary and returning fellow-citizens of mine) as large, as spacious and, above all, as precipitous as ever. Nor does the shock of contrast between its grey austerity, its abundant colour, its romantic aspect and its severely classical one grow less potent. It may be that Edinburgh in these respects is unique, stands alone amongst all cities in the British Isles, and for that matter elsewhere. It may be that those who leave it when young persuade themselves in the passing years that their dramatic and highly coloured memories of the place are no more than the usual self-delusions of youthful recollection, and that when they come back they are surprised by the accuracy of their memory, the reality of those indelible impressions they acquired so long ago. I don't know for certain. But I do know that Edinburgh has an unusually powerful way of imposing itself on the minds of children born and brought up in it.

Precipitous is one of Stevenson's favourite words about Edinburgh. Indeed, it comes into one of the last poems he wrote, the verse dedication of his last and unfinished book to his wife, written in the South Seas:

"I saw rain falling and the rainbow drawn
  On Lammermuir. Hearkening I heard again
  In my precipitous city beaten bells
  Winnow the keen sea wind..."

Precipitous, beaten bells, the keen sea wind, these are the words that occur to him naturally about Edinburgh when late at night (he composed these verses at night and pinned them to his wife's pillow so that she should see them in the morning), when late at night and late in his life his thoughts turned homewards. These words give a sense of height and space and sound and free air. They represent in all probability the first impressions of his surroundings that he had received as a child. There is nothing like approaching death (though he may not have been actively conscious of it) and a sense of physical distance for evoking the first thoughts and feelings of childhood.

To these early received yet lately recalled impressions of the town that saw his birth must be added the sense of contrast in which he revelled all his artistic life. Stevenson loved the clean cut of contrast in style and in subject matter. Jekyll and Hyde, the two brothers in *The Master of Ballantrae*, the many instances of his love of the clash of contrast in character, scenery and speech as well as innumerable other examples, all testify to this. But of all these the most celebrated and the most obvious is Jekyll and Hyde.

Dr. Jekyll and Mr. Hyde is far from being Stevenson's best book. Even amongst the generally educated reading public it is not his most celebrated. *Treasure Island* and *Kidnapped* lead the field. But if there is one single product of Stevenson's imagination that has impinged more than any other upon the mind of the world, it is undoubtedly Jekyll and Hyde. The two names in contrasting conjunction are familiar to people who have never read a word that Stevenson wrote, who know nothing about him, and to whom the initials R.L.S. have no meaning. This is not merely because the story is original and gripping and has been seized upon by stage and screen, making hundreds of thousands who can scarcely read, or scarcely be bothered to read, aware of it. No, the reason lies deeper. It is because, in this not wholly satisfying story (from the literary point of view), Stevenson said something eternally true that had never been said in fiction quite so explicitly or quite so nearly convincingly before. In one short novel of the thriller kind he anticipated a large part of the basis of modern psychology and had, at the same time, dipped far back and deep into the centuries-old secrets of moral theology.

All this about Jekyll and Hyde has been said before and often. But except for one penetrating paragraph in G. K. Chesterton's little study of Stevenson, and in a few scattered hints and asides in other biographies and essays, I do not think anyone has really accounted for the fact. There have been very few and unsatisfactory answers to the question of where he got it all from, of whence came this extraordinary conception so different from anything he had written or was to write. It is generally admitted that at the time of producing Jekyll and Hyde he had passed through experiences that had acted upon his mind and spirit as a kind of emetic. This may be true enough. And it certainly is interesting to speculate what it was that made the stomach of his imagination throw up this monstrosity of a tale that is already putting in a fair bid for immortality. What would be more interesting, would be to know where he acquired the stuff to make the vomit. No one will be able to answer that question fully now. But I do think that it is possible, while discussing the theme which is the subject of this study, to throw some light upon the problem.

The Strange Case of Dr. Jekyll and Mr. Hyde, to give it its full title, was conceived in a nightmare or at least in a thrilling dream. Mrs. R. L. Stevenson says that she was disturbed one night by her husband who was "uttering cries of horror in his sleep". When she woke him up to find out what the matter was he was indignant. "I was dreaming a fine bogey tale," he said, "and was just getting down to the details." In the morning he told her and his doctor who was then paying him a daily visit, "I've now *got* my shilling shocker." His publishers had been asking for a popular short book of late and he had replied evasively. After the dream, however, he had no desire to evade the subject but plunged into it with feverish gusto.

His fever was physical as well as mental, for he was running one of his pulmonary temperatures at the time. He wrote the first draft in three days in bed. The clinical thermometer was almost as frequently in his mouth as was the pencil in his hand. As the result of some frank, and probably well-founded, criticism from his wife, he became dissatisfied, not with the subject he was dealing with, but with his treatment of it. He at once burnt the draft completely, lest he should be tempted to start tinkering with it, and began again afresh. His bodily fever subsided, but the fever of his creative impulse remained. In three days it was rewritten, and, after a month of polishing and reflection it was ready for his publishers. It is not uncommon for imaginative writers to be seized by an uncontrollable longing to express a dream or a half-consciously conceived impulse. Sometimes the result is artistically worth while: often it is not. Always, if one is interested in the mind of the artist thus seized, it is worth studying. For what comes out of an experience of this kind reveals something that has been hidden in the man himself, either by his own will or by his circumstances.

At the time that Stevenson produced Jekyll and Hyde he had just passed through though not quite overcome the biggest crisis in his life. He had brought his long period of rebellion against the life that his family and the society had expected him to lead to a definite head. He had done it; and the very definiteness of his action was beginning to show results, if not complete success. It was many years since he had taken the first step which was to lead to this emancipation. It was many years since the "dreadful walk" with his father when he had announced that he would not follow the family calling of being a lighthouse engineer. But "they" had made him compromise and become an advocate at the Scottish bar. It was many years since he had said that, now that he had obeyed them by being called to that bar, he had no intention of pleading at it, but would devote his life to literature. Again, albeit with unusual kindness and forbearance, "they" had made him compromise. They had allowed him just enough freedom and resources to play with pen and paper and with the raw material of literature—experience, but had shown clearly enough that they had hoped that the end of this forbearance on their part would be his "coming to his senses" and his return to a respectable profession. It was many years since he had sought secret escape from these compromises imposed on him in "bohemian circles" and in love affairs outside the scope of his own society.

Now all that was over. The compromises were at an end. There was nothing secret. No one, not even his father, dreamed of suggesting that he should take up the family profession. The idea of his making a living at the Scottish bar was tacitly dropped as being obviously impracticable. His intention of becoming a professional writer was now accepted as an inevitable fact. He was actually making a little money by his pen. And, what was more important to himself, he was beginning to make a small name in the writing world. Finally, he had, in the matters pertaining to his own personal life, made one definite and complete rebellious action: and it had come off. He had run away to America without consulting his parents or anyone in Edinburgh, without more than a few pounds in his pocket, had married a divorced woman, had brought her back and had seen her received with decency and respect in his own home. If he cannot be said to have completely won his battle, the other side (and it was a side that, for all its opposition, he had loved and respected) had capitulated.

This capitulation had a number of results for him. It set him free in his personal life. It gave him a small measure of financial independence. It set him on his mettle to prove that, now that victory was in his reach, he could grasp it. It forced him to take up the challenge—the challenge of whether he really had it in him to be an artist by profession. And, and this is the point towards which I have been labouring, it ended his life in Edinburgh. He was to visit the city again. But he knew, and everyone else knew and accepted that it was no longer his home. The umbilical cord was cut.

The reasons for this severance were practical. First there was the overmastering one of health. Louis's lungs had always found the Edinburgh climate difficult to withstand. Now, after his grim experiences in America where his constitution had been further weakened by near starvation, everyone, doctors, family and friends realized that he could never seriously "put up his plate" in any professional capacity in his birthplace and settle down there. Then there was the question of his work, now an accepted vocation. It might have been all very well for an established writer to live in Scotland and issue his books through London publishers, but for a promising beginner like Louis it was obviously of advantage to him to be near the main source of his market. At the back of these practical reasons there was a less easily defined one which may well have weighed with the family as much as with R.L.S. himself. Edinburgh had been the scene of all Stevenson's early rebellions. It was in Edinburgh and from Edinburgh that the final capitulation of the family had come. Everyone in the small world of the

Stevenson society there knew it. If Louis were to fail in the course which had now been agreed upon, it would be the last humiliation—and a humiliation which had better take place furth of the town that had known his youth. If he were ever to return to Edinburgh for any length of time it had better be after he had succeeded.

But, success or no success, Stevenson must have known in his heart that the long Edinburgh phase of his life was over. It had been a phase of inescapable and deeply engraved memories, of romantic ardours and bitter disappointments, of a few ardent friendships and angry rebellion, of an intensely happy childhood and a storm-stressed youth, of first love and first frustration. They were memories as full of vivid contrast as was the city that had been their background. They were memories that were, so far from fading, to grow stronger with the passing years. But they were to be memories only; and he must have known it.

This, then, is the moment when Stevenson's subconsciousness chose to thrust up the concept of Jekyll and Hyde. It is as well to be wary of the facile use of the technicalities of modern psychiatry and to be careful of the easy explanations that they offer. But, when one recalls the extraordinary circumstances in which the story was thought of and written, as well as the time it was produced, it is surely not being too credulous to accept it as the explosion or release of some hidden part of Stevenson's mind.

The story of Jekyll and Hyde is supposed to be placed in London. But, as a number of critics have pointed out, there is a distinctly un-London flavour about it. Most of these critics have put this down to the dream-like origin and conception of the tale. They have thought that the background of the fantasy, with its strange "foreign atmosphere" was all a part of Stevenson's fantasy, and that it didn't exist. It does: it is Edinburgh. It was the London-born, wholly English-educated G. K. Chesterton who never saw Edinburgh until his middle life, who was the first to realize it. The moment I read this essay of Chesterton's (even though I was then scarcely more than an undergraduate considering myself wholly emancipated from my native city) I recognized its truth. This is no mere solitary impression. I have since put the point to a number of "Stevensonians" (unpleasant word, but unavoidable) who know Edinburgh. The reaction has always been the same. "Of course it's Edinburgh. Why didn't I realize it before?"

It would be tedious and ineffectual to try to analyse in detail an impression which, however true it may be, however widely recognized by intelligent and sensitive people, is no more than an impression. But Dr. Jekyll and Mr. Hyde's town *is* Edinburgh. The dark contrast between the dark evil and the almost equally ill-lit virtue is pure Edinburgh. The black old streets in which Hyde slinks on his evil path amidst carefully undescribed squalor and committing, for the most part, carefully unspecified sins, are Edinburgh streets. The heavily furnished, lamp-shaded interior of Dr. Jekyll's unostentatiously prosperous house is the inside of any well-to-do professional man's home in the New Town of Edinburgh. The contrast is not so much between black evil and golden goodness as between dark dirt and gloomy respectability. The stage throughout is only half lit. It is an Edinburgh Winter's Night tale.

Ill lit though the scene is the contrast between the good, the upright, the respectable on the one hand and the vile, the squalid, the vicious on the other, is savage and without subtlety—intentionally and effectively so. Its crudity is oddly naïve, like a child or very young person's conception of terrible utter badness and boring utter goodness. It is how a young man of imagination might view, in the abstract, the difference between an Edinburgh slum and an Edinburgh Christian merchant's home. There is no joy, fun or intoxication in either alternative, only a frenzied lust in the one and the dour satisfaction of an entrenched rectitude in the other. Along with the *Memoirs of a Justified Sinner* by Hogg (another writer who drew much of his inspiration from Edinburgh) it is one of the most savagely puritan, the most completely Calvinist products of the Scottish imaginative genius. And its background is Edinburgh.

Even the speech of the people in the story confirms this. Utterson the lawyer, Jekyll the alarming prig, even Hyde the abandoned evil-seeker, all speak with the elaborate but arresting old-fashioned precision, if not the accents of the Edinburgh upper classes. The poor people, the servants themselves seem to be speaking domestic Scotch translated into English. It is to be noted that this was a trick of dialogue which Stevenson used, either deliberately or unconsciously in other and later novels. The fantastic atmosphere of *The Wrong Box*, for instance, is heightened by the way in which the London and South of England characters talk. They give the air even in the most appalling and unlikely predicaments, of expressing themselves with a kind of racy eighteenth-century formality. It is not only eighteenth-century, it is Edinburgh. People talked like that in Edinburgh in Stevenson's day. Some "characters" in the city still do. However, in no other of his novels in an English or foreign setting do Stevenson's creations talk such obvious translated Edinburgh as in *Jekyll and Hyde*.

Of course *Jekyll and Hyde* is not an accurate picture of Edinburgh, nor anything like a just evocation of its atmosphere. What I have written in my earlier chapters will have been set down in vain if I have left the impression with the reader that I think of Edinburgh as a grand dramatic setting for the play and clash of joyless extremes. Of course there was a great deal of fun, and still is, in Edinburgh bohemianism, low life, or whatever you like to call it, even when it is not wicked or merely naughty. Of course there is much Christian joy in the decent homes of Edinburgh, in the practice of true piety within the city walls and within our city's convention.

And yet, it is possible to know what Stevenson meant, or half meant with his half-conscious dreams, when he thought of his native town as the setting for his most horrific tale. There are moods that attack the most devoted of Edinburgh's children when she seems to be nothing but the battleground between a frightening black and a depressing grey, when the inhabitants of her vivid slums are no longer vivid but only furtive and vile, when the respectable lose all their kindly humour and their deeply concealed, but at other times always perceptible latent emotionalism, and become mean, harsh and without humanity. There are times when the "haar", that peculiar Edinburgh silver grey, cold mist that the city sucks up from the Firth of Forth, rises and envelops her like a shroud. Sometimes it is possible to take a romantic view of the "haar", for there is a chilling beauty about it; sometimes it defeats even the most ardent lover of the town. He is conscious only that the Pentland Hills are blotted out, that the Castle is obscured, the streets reduced to uniform dull channels of moist air. At such times it is not difficult for him to imagine that behind those tightly-drawn, thick, heavy curtains, there is sitting over his books and his medical instruments the repellent Dr. Jekyll, or that that figure in the mist just ahead of him, slinking into the convenient slum, is really Mr. Hyde.

Having got *The Strange Case of Dr. Jekyll and Mr. Hyde* out of his system, Stevenson easily sloughed what he fancied were the Edinburgh remains of Hyde in him. Fancied is the operative word; for anything less like Hyde's joyless lust for evil than Louis's romantically inspired wanderings in the under and bohemian world of Leith Walk and Lothian Road can hardly be imagined. Unfortunately, but in the circumstances understandably, he did not get rid of Jekyll so easily—I say understandably because his family's generous capitulation, his wife's strenuous efforts to be worthy of that capitulation touched him, as well as inspired him to respectability. Respectability, a settled background and the presence about him of people who believed in him as well as loved him, were exactly what he needed at this time. It is not at all strange that in his thankfulness for these things, he reacted a little too favourably towards the Jekyll background of his youth, not so much the loving, decent background of his family, as the Edinburgh respectability against which he had rebelled. There was always a morally sententious streak in him, as there is in nearly every Edinburgh Scot—see his lamentable essay on Burns—but after the publication of *Jekyll and Hyde*, and the ensuing success of his literary life, this sententiousness came a trifle more easily to him. It seemed less an affectation of youth and more natural. Henley, who knew him so well and loved him so well in youth, had included the line "Something of the Shorter Catechist" in his famous and affectionate sonnet in early days. Henley, who still loved him, but with a bitter, thwarted, possessive jealousy to the end of his life, was to use the same phrase as a jeer in his savage review of Graham Balfour's biography after Stevenson's death. Making all allowances for Henley's tortured temperament, one must admit that he had something to support his unnecessary and untimely jeer, when one examines some of R.L.S.'s later writings.

Ah, but it is easy to be unfair about all this. Stevenson's moral sententiousness was not real Jekyllism. It had none of that bitter rectitude about it which we associate with Jekyll's kind. It may have been no more than the half-conscious expression of gratitude towards those who had helped, loved him, believed in him and protected him—precisely those, it must be remembered, of whom Henley was so jealous. It may have been more a justification of the way of life of those who surrounded him, than self-justification. And though he had sloughed off the fancied Edinburgh Hyde (the imaginary evil character), the reality behind that Hyde, the eager-eyed youth, avid for the honey of low life, remained somewhere in him, hidden, but far from quiescent. He was always sympathetic to young people who showed the same avidity. He could always be roused to fury by what he believed to be hypocrisy. It may have been this that was at the back of his mind when he admitted later on to having a sneaking fondness for Hyde.

But as he drew towards the end of his life, both Jekyll and Hyde faded from his imagination. Separated by years and distance from the city that had given him birth, that had provoked from him, in immediate recollection, this fantastic explosion of a story, he began to see it whole and not in part, more clearly and with greater steadiness. The nostalgia for Edinburgh, for its sights, sounds and people that he expressed with such poignancy in his last books and poems, is not sentimental. It is not (to use the cant phrase) the product of looking at the past through rose-coloured spectacles, but of clear and loving vision. The proof of this is that in all English or Scots literature there exists nothing more truly evocative of the real Edinburgh than Stevenson's last writings.

CHAPTER IX

STEVENSON wrote one short book entirely about Edinburgh, his *Edinburgh; Picturesque Notes*. It is well named; for it is not a guide book but a collection of the very well-informed personal reflections of a still comparatively young writer on his native city. It was written abroad, while Stevenson was in a fairly happy condition; and he looks back, while on a prolonged holiday, and from the dizzy heights of twenty-eight, on Edinburgh with a guarded affection. He was very much on his best behaviour when he was writing the *Picturesque Notes*, and was careful not to hint at any of his deeper personal feelings about the place. Though some of his remarks about the inhabitants caused Victorian eyebrows to rise, particularly the following:

"The feeling grows upon you that this also is a piece of nature in the most intimate sense; that this profusion of eccentricities, this dream in masonry and living rock, is not a drop-scene in a theatre, but a city in the world of everyday reality, connected by railway and telegraph-wire with all the capitals of Europe, and inhabited by citizens of the familiar type, who keep ledgers, and attend church, and have sold their immortal portion to a daily paper. By all the canons of romance, the place demands to be half deserted and leaning towards decay; birds we might admit in profusion, the play of the sun and winds, and a few gipsies encamped in the chief thoroughfare; but these citizens, with their cabs and tramways, their trains and posters, are altogether out of key. Chartered tourists, they make free with historic localities, and rear their young among the most picturesque sites with a grand human indifference. To see them thronging by, in their neat clothes and conscious moral rectitude, and with a little air of possession that verges on the absurd, is not the least striking feature of the place."

But on the whole the book passed muster even amongst the respectable circles of Edinburgh of 1878. What is more important is that it still passes muster to-day. The charm of its careful, yet enthusiastic, perhaps slightly mannered prose still works. It remains, moreover, one of the best and truest pieces of writing on Edinburgh in the language—one, but not *the* best—that was to come, and from the same pen. Its excellence is attested by the fact that it is still bought and read, not only because it is by R.L.S. but because it describes so well the atmosphere and appearance of Edinburgh to those who are curious about her, and evokes them for those who know the city, but who are away from her. This, it must be admitted, is partly due to Edinburgh's celebrated immutability. Had, let us say, Dickens written a similar book on the atmosphere, appearance and topography of London about the same date, it might have been a work of art, and certainly a literary and social curiosity. It would equally certainly not be bought and read half way through the twentieth century by Londoners and visitors as an accurate book about modern London.

I began this book by asking the reader to place himself in imagination on the top of the Calton Hill at the East End of Princes Street, and to survey the modern city below him. "Of all places for a view this Calton Hill is perhaps the best," says R.L.S. in the *Picturesque Notes*. He continues in his admirable chapter on the Calton Hill to describe what the view from there is, reaching a climax in the well-known passage:

> "These are the main features of the scene roughly sketched. How they are all tilted by the inclination of the ground, how each stands out in delicate relief against the rest, what manifold detail, and play of sun and shadow, animate and accentuate the picture, is a matter for a person on the spot, and turning swiftly on his heels, to grasp and bind together in one comprehensive look. It is the character of such a prospect, to be full of change and of things moving. The multiplicity embarrasses the eye; and the mind, among so much, suffers itself to grow absorbed with single points. You remark a tree in a hedgerow, or follow a cart along a country road. You turn to

the city, and see children, dwarfed by distance into pigmies, at play about suburban doorsteps; you have a glimpse upon a thoroughfare where people are densely moving; you note ridge after ridge of chimney-stacks running downhill one behind another, and church spires rising bravely from the sea of roofs. At one of the innumerable windows, you watch a figure moving; on one of the multitude of roofs, you watch clambering chimney-sweeps. The wind takes a run and scatters the smoke; bells are heard, far and near, faint and loud, to tell the hour; or perhaps a bird goes dipping evenly over the housetops, like a gull across the waves. And here you are in the meantime, on this pastoral hillside, among nibbling sheep and looked upon by monumental buildings."

In my first chapter I also imagined Stevenson himself standing beside the spectator and myself looking down on the city of to-day. I wondered what he would feel and say were I to be able to take him down from the heights which he knew so well, which have changed so little since his day, and to introduce him to the streets, the houses and the people of Edinburgh one hundred years after his birth. I end this book by allowing myself in imagination the luxury of such an expedition.

I would begin by taking him to my house in Inverleith Row almost opposite to his own birthplace at 8 Howard Place. We would come down by a route very familiar to him. We would touch the East End of Princes Street by the Register House, turn down Leith Street and Broughton Street past the Catholic Cathedral, over the Water of Leith by Canonmills and thus home. His main impression, I think, would be how little this part of the town had changed. I pass over the obvious shocks of novelty such as the electric tram cars, the congested traffic, the crowded pavements in our glimpse of Princes Street, the women's fashions, and so on, as hardly worth mentioning. We should spend about five minutes while I explained these things to him. Then, I think, save for an occasional question and answer, we would leave them alone. One purely factual modern thing might take him aback, however. I would not be able to refrain from taking him into "the Northern Bar" at the corner of Howard Place and Warriston Crescent, his "local" until the age of five, and a public house he may well have visited from Heriot Row later on, when of a drinking age. I would, of course, stand him a glass of whisky. His curious mind, always inquisitive about figures of money, would be, I am sure, appalled by the fact that I would have to pay five shillings for what cost fourpence or sixpence in his day. It would be particularly poignant if I were to have to pay for his drink with two half-crowns bearing the effigy of his own Sovereign Queen Victoria.

When I had got him home I should take him to the room in which I am writing these words. For all I know he may have been in it before. He would find it more sparsely and cleanly furnished than in his day; but the late protracted Georgian 1840 proportions of it would evoke a memory in him. I would take him to my windows where he could look out on to the Botanic Gardens, his resort as a child and a young man. He would not notice much difference. Then, leaning out of those windows he would be able to catch a glimpse of the grand silhouette of the Castle and its rock—unchanged, and in the distance of his own "Hills of Home", the Pentlands—eternal. He would, I think, be gladdened by all this.

What should I do with him then—presuming always that it was my duty to entertain and inform him about our Edinburgh and not to extract knowledge from him about his town? Well, I should ask him to sit in my room where he could look out on to the views of his own childhood and try to tell him a little bit about Edinburgh a hundred years after he had been born just across the way. I would avoid the subject of his own centenary, his posthumous fame, for somehow, I think he would probably know all about that. Nor would I wish to embarrass him by raising the subject of the R.L.S. cult and the Cummy cult when they were at their height at the time of my boyhood. In the shades he would probably have heard about those things too. I would, however, show him my wireless box and tell him that there came out of it at intervals readings from his own books and poems, and dramatized versions of his stories. I would not mention the talks about him; but I would say that all this came from the Scottish B.B.C. in Edinburgh.

"The Scottish B.B.C.?" he would ask.

"Yes," I would reply, and tell him all about it.

"Shall we go there?" he might ask wistfully.

"No, I think not. It's all right for me, but I think you would be a bit puzzled and embarrassed. But listen to this."

Then I would turn on some music, Mozart for preference. Then, if the time was propitious, I would let him hear some Scottish country dance music.

"Good Heavens," he would say, "in my day that sort of tune used to be kept only to the country bothies and that sort of place. Do people listen to it in Edinburgh?"

"Yes, and like it, though how many people dance to it I don't know." Then, becoming rather enthusiastically informative about my own hobbyhorse, because I would want to know his reaction, I would add, "And there's all sorts of other things that come out of this box, news in Gaelic, Gaelic lessons, even."

"Gaelic in Edinburgh. Good God!"

"Yes, and plays and talks in and about Lallans and . . ."

Here he would interrupt me with an incredulous laugh. "Lallans! but Good Lord! I invented that word."

"No you didn't. It was . . ."

"You're perfectly right. I'm sorry. It was Burns or Fergusson, or . . ."

"Burns was the one who really brought the word out into the open, though Fergusson knew it and probably used it."

"Fergusson," he would say, and then fall silent for a bit. "Is he still remembered?"

"He certainly is. It was your own writings about him seventy to eighty years ago that revived the interest in him. It has never stopped. It has grown."

"I hope they're going to remember his birthday, his bi-centenary too, this year?" He would smile in his eager way as he asked this question.

"They certainly are. Indeed," I would go on after a pause, "some fanciful people are wondering if there is going to be another Robert born in Edinburgh this year. Robert Fergusson in 1750, Robert Louis Balfour Stevenson in 1850 and Robert . . . well, Robert Someone in 1950."

"But do you think that Edinburgh is still enough Edinburgh, enough *of* Edinburgh to make a poet out of herself nowadays? After all, you've been telling me about the British wireless, the motor-cars, the aeroplanes and so on (we do hear about these things in the shades, you know), the world's becoming a small place. Great Britain is a tiny island, aren't people talking the same all over it? Does Edinburgh really remain Edinburgh? Is it capable of . . . of . . .?"

"I think it is," I would say firmly. And then I would ride my hobby-horse again. I would tell him about Scottish Nationalism in politics, in social life, in the arts, and above all in his own art of words. I would tell him of the young men, and the not so young men who are feeling, and have felt for twenty years, the compulsion to express Scotland, their own country of Scotland, through Scottish verse and prose. I would, with some diffidence, but as clearly as I could, try to tell him about the Lallans writers and poets who half laugh at themselves but entirely believe in themselves. I would tell him of the controversies they have aroused. I could not refrain from adding that those who have most bitterly opposed them are precisely the same kind of people who laughed at him in Edinburgh when he was alive. Hastily forestalling a question I would admit that beyond a few phrases of Gaelic I have no knowledge of the language at all, and that I would hesitate to write anything save reported dialogue in Lallans, myself. But I would affirm that I knew enough about the Scottish tongue *and* about poetry to be sure that some of what these young enthusiasts are writing is not only true Scots, but true poetry. I would end by telling him that, with all failings and all laughable absurdities, I believed in the new Scotland and the new Edinburgh which is the capital of it.

He would smile, of course, but with sympathy as well as curiosity, I think. Then he would say:

"Let's go out and see it . . . some of them."

We would go out. I would take him to a certain howff in Rose Street which he might have remembered in the old days. But I would insist on going there by way of a detour through the noblest parts of the New Town, just to show him how magnificently unchanged it all was. He would be a little bit surprised at my enthusiasm for this, one of the noblest relics of the eighteenth century left in Western Europe; for the New Town was not much regarded in his day. Our dispute or discussion over the merits of Moray Place, Charlotte Square and his own Heriot Row would lead us to prolong our detour into the heights of the Old Town. Here we would be at one. He would be pleased to notice what care my generation has taken of the structure and shape of this historic part, the genuine and loving industry with which some old houses have been restored to their ancient dignity. And, *nostalgie de la boue* or no *nostalgie de la boue*, I am sure he would be pleased that these districts are slightly less horrific than in his day. Eventually (having explained to him the cruel necessity of obeying our modern licensing laws) I would lead him down the Mound to an appropriately named tavern in the New Town.

Here my imagination takes wings. I would fill the place with everyone whom I should wish him to meet. He would be delighted by the gaunt eccentricity of Douglas Young the Scottish poet and scholar; his humorous pedantry, and genuine flashes of poetic feeling alternating with it, would please him enormously. He might even learn some neologistic Lallanisms from him—"faur speaker" for telephone, for instance! He would not be in the least upset by the violent disagreements in argument which C. M. Grieve (Hugh MacDiarmid) would try to provoke, for he would recognize not only the essential amiability, but the Shelley-like flame of poetry that burns in the little man. Compton Mackenzie would be there on a visit from the Hebrides or from the south. R.L.S. would be a little suspicious of him until they had met. Then they would at once fall victims to each other's charm. And they would not be in the least jealous of each other. "It is a pity that Cunninghame Grahame isn't here," I would apologize, "but he is . . . er . . . dead."

"Yes, yes, I know," R.L.S. would rebuke me. "I knew him, or at least I knew of him. I know him now, of course."

He would meet the Gaelic poets and writers, the younger painters, the rather pawky elder journalists in the movement. And by some terrific feat of my imagination I should induce some of the old guard of eccentrics and fighters in the Scottish cause to enter the tavern. He would be quite enchanted by "the Major". In short, I quite honestly believe that, in their differing ways, he would like them all. Though what he would think of me, I haven't the faintest idea.

Then in order that his ears might not be affronted by the hideous clangour of the electric bell that goes for "closing time", I would slip him away from the party while it was still at its height. I should take him back to where we started, the top of the Calton

Hill to say good-bye. As we looked down on the dimly illuminated city—still dimly illuminated after a hundred years—I should not be able to refrain from asking him:

"Well, have I convinced you that your Edinburgh still remains?"

He would smile and evade the question.

"I've thoroughly enjoyed myself."

"Yes, but have I convinced you?"

"Perhaps, perhaps. But ... but have you convinced *yourself*?"

It would then be my turn to pause. After a while I would admit, "perhaps, perhaps."

And with those words ringing in my mind I would release him from my imagination, and from the Edinburgh of a hundred years after his birth. With those words, too, as an undertone to all I have written here, I end this book on Stevenson and Edinburgh? Edinburgh and Stevenson?